HANDGUNS

HANDGUNS

Jim Supica

T&J

Produced by TAJ Books International LLP
27, Ferndown Gardens,
Cobham,
Surrey,
UK,
KT11 2BH
www.tajbooks.com

Company history text supplied by Karen Vellucci

Photo courtesy Jim Supica, ArmchairGunShow.com
pages 6, 7, 8, 9, 10, 11 (both), 12, 13, 14, 15, 16 (both), 17, 18, 19 (both), 20

You can join the NRA by contacting them at:

The National Rifle Association of America
11250 Waples Mill Road
Fairfax VA 22030

or by visiting their website, www.nra.org

And you can view the treasures of the NRA National Firearms Museum at the website
www.nramuseum.org.

The museum is open every day of the week, except major holidays, at NRA Headquarters in Fairfax VA, near
Washington DC. There is no admission charge.

All notations of errors or omissions should be addressed to Thunder Bay Press, Editorial Department, at the
above address. All other correspondence (author inquiries, permissions) concerning the content of this book
should be addressed to TAJ Books, 27, Ferndown Gardens, Cobham, Surrey, UK, KT11 2BH, info@tajbooks.com.

ISBN-13: 978-1-84406-148-8

Library of Congress Cataloging-in-Publication Data available on request.

Printed in China.

3 4 5 14 13 12

CONTENTS

Introduction

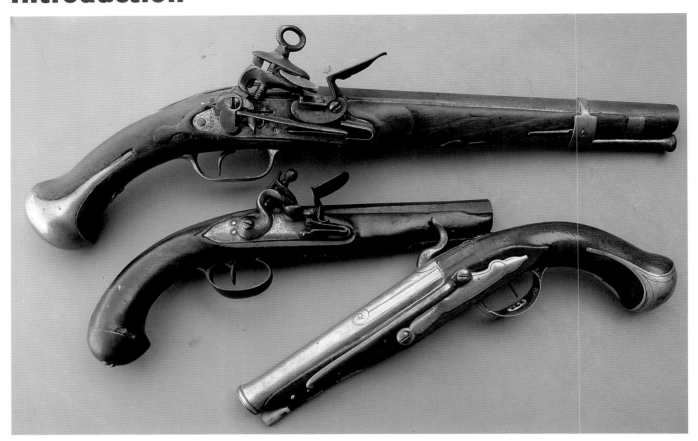

Early muzzleloading firearms ignition systems included the Miquelet form of flintlock, shown on the Spanish pistol, ca. 1700s (top); the perfected flintlock system shown on the American flintlock pistol (middle); and the percussion system as used on the brass barrel French pistol, ca. mid-1800s (bottom).

A Brief History of Firearms

As long as man has used tools, weapons have been among those of foremost importance. They have been used to provide food and protection since the formation of the earliest social units.

For centuries, and continuing through today, men and women have used firearms as the most effective weapons individuals can wield. Guns have been used to implement both the highest and basest goals of humanity: to put food on the table, to provide personal protection, to enforce or defy the law, to defend or acquire territory and treasure, and to liberate or to enslave.

Guns have also come to be used for a wide variety of recreational and competitive shooting, and millions of Americans exercise their constitutional right to own firearms simply for the pleasure of shooting or the enjoyment of ownership.

The Handgun

A "handgun" is generally a firearm that is fired, controlled, and stabilized in shooting using only the hands. This differs from long guns (rifles and shotguns), which have stocks that are braced against the shooter's shoulder for added stability and accuracy when aiming and firing. Nearly all handguns are capable of being fired one-handed, although modern technique will usually use two hands for additional control.

Of course handguns are smaller than long guns, with shorter barrels, and grips instead of a buttstock. In the United States there are important legal differences between handguns, rifles, and shotguns, due to heavy restrictions and licensing requirements on guns considered to be "short-barreled rifles" or "short-barreled shotguns." To avoid breaking this law, a handgun will have a barrel shorter than 16 inches, and an overall length of less than 24 inches. The vast majority are significantly smaller than that, with common barrel lengths running 2 inches to 8 inches or so. It also must have a rifled bore, as smoothbore

handguns are considered short-barreled shotguns, and are highly restricted.

The primary purpose of a handgun is to be handy. There are few shooting tasks that a shotgun or rifle will not perform better than a handgun in terms of accuracy and power, but the handgun has the virtue of being convenient—easily carried leaving the hands free, and concealed if dictated by circumstances or required by law. It can be carried for use if needed, and is out of the way and not a burden if it is not. It can be available in circumstances where a rifle or shotgun could not.

Earliest Firearms

The origin of gunpowder is unknown, and may have occurred in China, Turkey, or Europe. The first record describing the combination of charcoal, sulphur, and saltpeter, to produce a rapidly burning or exploding powder is a coded writing by Franciscan monk Roger Bacon shortly before 1250 AD.

Within fifty years, early cannons had been developed. A large, thick metal tube with one closed end (the breech) and an open end (the muzzle) was loaded first with gunpowder and then with a projectile. The powder was ignited with a torch or smoldering ember through a small hole in the rear (the touch hole). The rapidly expanding gases from the exploding gunpowder would throw the projectile from the barrel. This basic principle still applies today.

It took another half century for this concept to be applied to individual handheld weapons. The first firearms, ca. 1350, called "hand cannons" or "hand gonnes" were essentially miniature cannons designed to be held by hand or attached to a pole for use by individual soldiers. They were loaded and fired in the same manner as the full-size cannons.

Early Ignition Systems

For the next four centuries, the greatest advances in the evolution of firearms would focus primarily on the search for more reliable methods of igniting the gunpowder, in addition to design advances for more rapid repeat shots and better accuracy.

The term "lock, stock, and barrel" comes from firearms design, representing the three major components of early guns. The barrel is self-explanatory, and the stock is of course the wooden holder in which the barrel is mounted, allowing the gun to be fired from the shoulder or from one hand. The lock is the mechanical contrivance that is used to ignite the charge of gunpowder in the chamber of the barrel.

The first gun to combine all three components was the matchlock, in the early 1400s. Many early hand cannons were ignited with a "slow match" – a length of slender rope or cord that had been chemically treated so that an end could be ignited and would continue to burn or smolder, much like a punk used to shoot fireworks. Obviously it was awkward to hold both gun & slow match while trying to dip the match to the touch hole of the hand cannon.

The matchlock solved this problem by using an arm called a serpentine on the gun to hold the slow match. By mechanical linkage, a trigger mounted on the bottom of the lock could be pressed to lower the match to the touch hole, which now included a small pan of fine gunpowder that would be ignited first, transmitting the fire through the hole to fire the main charge in the barrel.

This simple system was followed by a much more complicated one, the wheellock in the early 1500s. It was the first to take advantage of the fact that sparks could be produced by striking flint or other

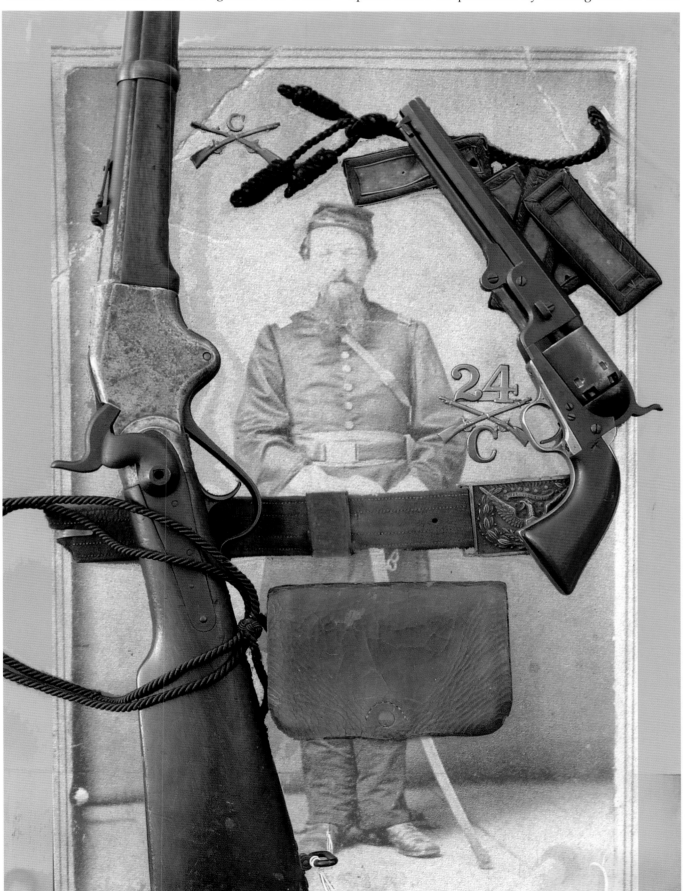

The American Civil War was a time of rapid evolution in firearms design. Shown here are a Colt 1851 Navy revolver and Spencer repeating carbine, both used by Captain William Weston of the 7th Kansas Volunteers.

Introduction

Smith & Wesson introduced the first commercially successful revolver to fire a self-contained metallic cartridge with its Model One in the mid-nineteenth century. Shown here is a very rare pair of consecutive numbered factory engraved Model Ones, with an original gutta-percha case.

substances against steel. The lock contained a wheel with a serrated edge, attached to a spring that could be wound with a separate key called a spanner, much like early clocks, and held under tension. A hammer-like piece called the dogshead held a piece of pyrite rock. To fire a wheellock, the dogshead was lowered onto the edge of the wheel, which was released by a pull of the trigger causing a shower of sparks to fall into the pan and igniting the charge. The principle is much the same as a cigarette lighter.

This was an improvement in reliability over the matchlock, primarily because the shooter did not have to constantly attend to the smoldering slow match to ensure that it remained lit. It also avoided the problem of an enemy seeing—or game smelling—the smoke of the match before the gun was fired. However, it took highly skilled craftsmen to build the clocklike mechanism of the wheellock, making it an extremely expensive piece, primarily available to royalty and the like for hunting. Although wheellocks saw some military use, the matchlock remained the most common military firearm during the wheellock era.

One of today's premier handgun makers can trace its roots to this era. Beretta began operations in Brescia, Italy, in 1526, making it one of the oldest industrial companies in the world.

Flintlocks

Improvements using flint against steel to provide the igniting spark continued in the second half of the sixteenth century, with two early examples being the snaphaunce, the first flintlock-type gun ca. 1560, and the Miquelet, following a couple decades later.

The snaphaunce held a piece of flint in the hammer-like cock, with a pan of priming powder mounted on the outside of the barrel over the touch hole as with the matchlock system. When ready to fire, a steel striking plate (the "battery") would be manually swiveled into place above the pan, and the cock pulled back until it was caught by a sear. Pulling the trigger would release the cock to swing rapidly forward, striking the battery and showering sparks into the pan, hopefully firing the gun.

As with all flintlock-type systems, sometimes the priming powder in the pan would ignite, but would fail to transmit the fire to the powder in the barrel resulting in a failure to fire, and giving us a colorful phrase still used today: "a flash in the pan."

Of course, it was also vital to "keep your powder dry," and accordingly many early firearms of this era had a sliding pan cover to hold the powder in place and give it some protection against the elements. The pan cover would have to be manually swiveled out of the way before firing.

Around 1580 the Miquelet system improved on and simplified the snaphaunce by combining the battery and pan cover into a single piece, called the frizzen. This L-shaped spring-loaded piece would be pivoted down to cover the pan after it had been primed with powder. When the cock was released by the trigger, it would swing forward striking the frizzen, producing sparks at the same time it pushed the frizzen up and forward to expose the powder in the pan to the igniting sparks.

In the early 1600s, the basic design of the flintlock, originally known as the French lock, was perfected. The major improvement over the Miquelet consisted of moving the mechanical components for the lock mechanism from their previous position on the outside of the lockplate, where they were exposed to elements and damage to the interior of the lock.

Improvements In Accuracy

At around the time flintlock systems were first being developed, two improvements were introduced that dramatically increased the accuracy of firearms. Archers had found that if the fletching feathers on the rear of their arrow were at a slight angle, causing the arrow to rotate in flight, their ability to hit the target was improved. This concept was applied to gun barrels by cutting slightly twisting grooves down the interior length of the barrel, imparting a spin to the bullet as it left the muzzle. These grooves were called rifling, and rifled guns were found to be much better at hitting their mark over farther distances than those with "smooth bores."

With the improved accuracy offered by rifled firearms, a system of aiming them other than pointing became more important, and early forms of sights became more widely used. A common system, still used on most handguns today, was a notch of some type at the rear of the barrel and a post on the front. With this type of open sight, the top of the front sight post is aligned with the target, and the post is centered by eye between the edges of the rear sight notch, with the top of the post level with the tops of the sides of the notch. When the sights themselves are properly physically aligned with the axis of the bore, this system still provides all the accuracy required for most practical shooting needs.

Each of these early forms of firearms can be found in both handgun and long gun configurations.

The Percussion System

Although the flintlock system predominated in firearms production for nearly two centuries, problems remained. A shooter often had to carry two types of powder—fine grained for priming and coarse for the main charge, and the system was unreliable in wet weather. It was difficult to store a gun loaded and ready for use.

In 1807 a Scottish clergyman, Reverand Alexander John Forsyth, is credited with developing an ignition system based on the principle that certain chemicals would ignite with a spark when struck with a sharp blow—a concept which can be observed in toy cap pistols or "pop rock" fireworks today. Various methods to utilize this approach were tried, and in 1822 the percussion cap was invented.

The percussion cap contains a small charge of chemical in a small copper cuplike holder that can be quickly pressed onto to a nipple mounted in the rear of a gun barrel. When the trigger is pulled, the hammer strikes the cap, igniting the chemical, which sparks through a hole in the nipple into the main charge in the barrel, firing the gun. This system offered such obvious advantages to the flintlock method that gunmakers around the world rapidly adapted their existing designs to percussion ignition, although within fifty years of accelerating firearms evolution, it too, would be obsolete.

Both flintlock and percussion handguns were made in a wide range of sizes. They ranged from massive "horse pistols," very large pieces, intended to be primarily carried in holsters attached to the saddle, to small "pocket pistols" suitable for a gentleman's

Guns closely associated with the Old West include the Colt single action army (top), the Sharps buffalo rifle (middle), and "hideout" guns such as the Smith & Wesson Model One (bottom).

Introduction

Fancy engraved firearms were highly prized in the late 1800s. Shown here are a factory-engraved Colt 1877 Double Action Lightning revolver in .38 caliber, and its larger companion, a scroll-engraved Colt 1878 Double Action in .44-40 caliber. Pearl and ivory grips were considered deluxe embellishments, appropriate for such finely decorated sidearms.

pocket, or "muff pistols" concealable in a lady's hand warmer for personal protection. One maker of small pistols was so successful and prominent that his name came to be used as a generic term for small hideout handguns—Henry Deringer of Philadelphia. His small size of pistol has picked up the nickname of "peanut." His popularity was such that other makers would mark their guns with slight variations of his name, such as "Derringer," hoping to fool unwary buyers. It is this latter spelling, derringer, that is still used today.

The Revolver

The introduction of the percussion system marks the beginning of a dramatically rapid era of firearms advancements, coinciding with the Industrial Revolution and including the era of the American Civil War, through the turn of the century. During this relatively brief time, guns would go from primitive flintlocks to the basic systems that still dominate firearms designs today.

At the beginning of the percussion era, a pressing concern was the relatively long time it took to reload a firearm, and the need for rapid follow-up shots. An archer could loose several arrows in the time it took a pistolero to pour a charge of powder down the barrel, ram home a ball, and seat a primer on the nipple between shots.

In the earliest days of firearms design, this could be addressed in a limited manner by mounting multiple barrels (and usually multiple locks) onto the same stock. However, with more than two barrels, the system begins to become heavy and cumbersome. Other systems were tried, including manually rotated groups of barrels mounted to a single lock, multiple superposed charges within a single barrel, and cylindrical or rectangular clusters of chambers which could be manually repositioned to align with a firing mechanism and barrel.

The most successful solution was invented by Samuel Colt. He developed a handgun design with a rotating cylinder with multiple chambers, each of which could contain a charge of powder topped by the bullet, loaded from the front of the cylinder. The rear of the cylinder was closed, with a nipple for a percussion cap installed at the back of each chamber. When the hammer is cocked, a fresh chamber rotates into alignment with the rear of the barrel, and when the trigger is pulled the hammer drops, firing the load

Remington was a major handgun manufacturer in the mid-nineteenth century. Clockwise from top left: large-frame single shot Rolling Block pistol; large-frame Model 1875 Single Action Army .44 caliber revolver; rare Remington Beals 1st Model Pocket Percussion Revolver, the firm's first revolver ca. 1857; unusual Remington Rider magazine pistol ca. 1871–88; and a rare Remington Rider Zig-Zag barrel pepperbox derringer.

in that chamber. This is the basis of the mechanical system still used in all revolvers today.

Colt's first manufacturing venture was based in Paterson, New Jersey, and produced percussion revolvers with folding triggers. These are called Colt Paterson models by modern collectors. Relatively few were produced, and the firm folded, having been in business only from 1837 to 1841. Their importance in firearms evolution, and their scarcity, make them highly prized collectors' items. When a specimen in good condition appears on the market, the price can be in the six figures.

The idea was too good to die, and in 1847 Colt was back with a new, heavier, more powerful revolver, this time with a traditional bow type trigger guard. Prompted by an initial order from Captain Samuel Walker to equip his troops in the Mexican-American

War, the new model tipped the scales at nearly five pounds, and remained the most powerful repeating handgun until the introduction of the .357 magnum nearly ninety years later. It was called the Walker Model, after the young captain. Colt's revolvers were initially manufactured by Eli Whitney, but Colt soon had his own plant in Hartford, Connecticut.

Colt had patented his revolving cylinder design, and so held a monopoly on revolver manufacture for a number of years. The only serious competition for a repeating handgun was the pepperbox design, in which a cluster of barrels, each with a percussion nipple on the rear, rotated around an axis by the pull of a ring trigger, which also cocked the hammer and released it to fire the chamber which had rotated into position. Pepperboxes were made by a number of European and American firms, the foremost probably

Smith & Wesson's reputation for exceptional revolvers continued into the twentieth century, with models ranging from the large .44 Special "Triple Lock" target hand ejector (ca. 1907–15) through the diminutive .22 "Lady Smith" (ca. 1902–21).

Smith & Wesson was the predominant revolver manufacturer of the nineteenth century post–Civil War. Some of its products shown here include (clockwise from top left) New Model Number 3 single action .44 revolver (1878–1912); engraved Model Two Old Army (1861–74); engraved .38 Double Action (1880–1911); and engraved Model One-and-a-half (1865–75).

being the succession of companies founded by Ethan Allen, including Allen & Thurber and Allen & Wheelock.

The Colt pattern cap and ball revolver rapidly came to dominate the repeating firearms market however, with Colt offering revolving shotguns and rifles as well as handguns. Among his most successful designs were the little 1849 Pocket Model in .31 caliber, the midsized 1851 Navy Model in .36 caliber, and the 1861 Army Model, offering .44 caliber chambering in a much smaller and handier package than his earlier Walker and Dragoon models. After the expiration of Colt's patent in the mid-1850's, other firms jumped into the revolver business, with major manufacturers including Remington, Starr, Whitney, and Manhattan. From these and other makers, the percussion revolver was the major sidearm of the Civil War.

The Self-Contained Cartridge

The cap and ball revolver offered an effective repeating firearm, with five or six shots available as fast as the hammer could be cocked and the trigger pulled. After the gun was shot dry, however, reloading was a slow and cumbersome process, involving loading each chamber with loose gun powder and a lead bullet, ramming the loads home, and placing a percussion cap on the nipple of each chamber. What was needed was a self-contained cartridge with the primer, powder, and bullet all in one neat and weatherproof unit.

An early attempt at this was the pinfire system, first introduced around 1846, in which a firing pin was mounted on each copper-cased cartridge, igniting an internal primer when struck by the gun's hammer. Although it gained a good deal of popularity in Europe, it never caught on much in the United States, with the external pin on each round being a bit cumbersome and hazardous.

Among the firms eagerly waiting for the expiration of the Colt revolver patent was a partnership of an inventor named Daniel Wesson and an older businessman, Horace Smith. A few years earlier, in a previous partnership, they had entered the race for an effective repeating firearm shooting self-contained cartridges with a lever-action pistol. This pistol had a tubular magazine mounted under and parallel to the barrel, and shot "rocket balls"—hollow-based lead bullets, with the powder and primer mounted in the base of the projectile itself.

They pursued production of their lever-action pistols only a few years, and the design was acquired by a shirt manufacturer, who carried it further. His name was Oliver Winchester, and his famous lever-action rifles, based in large part on the design of the first Smith & Wesson partnership, eventually became the most popular repeating rifles of the post–Civil War nineteenth century, called by many "the gun that won the West."

The second Smith & Wesson partnership, had designed a tiny .22 revolver. Perhaps more important than the revolver was the cartridge it fired. It consisted of a copper casing, with a hollow rim at the bottom that held a priming compound. The case was then filled with gunpowder, and capped with a lead bullet mounted into its mouth. When the firing pin of the revolver's hammer struck the rim of the cartridge, the priming ignited the powder, firing the bullet, leaving the empty copper casing in the chamber. The cartridge was essentially identical to the modern .22 Short rimfire, and was the granddaddy of all our traditional ammunition today.

As Colt had patented his revolver, so Smith & Wesson acquired the patent to their innovation, and held a fairly complete monopoly on the production of effective cartridge revolvers through its expiration in 1869, although there were a number of infringements and evasions of the patent as the market rapidly recognized the superiority of metallic cartridge ammunition.

The American West

The American West of 1865 to 1900 is perhaps one of the most popular and romanticized eras of American history, with the lore of cowboy and Indian, lawman and outlaw, figuring large in our collective imagination. The handguns of this era also have a special fascination.

The most famous is undoubtedly the Colt Single Action Army, introduced in 1873, and also known as the Peacemaker. Its sturdy reliable design and effective cartridges made it a favorite with Westerners on both sides of the law.

It is little recognized, however, that Smith & Wesson large-frame top-break revolvers and their foreign copies represented the most prolific full-size handgun pattern of the early cartridge era. All variations were based on the Model Three frame, the first was the American model in 1870, followed rapidly by the Russian model. The Schofield model was made for the American military in the 1870s, followed by the New Model Number Three and Double Action models.

The Smith & Wesson design was much faster to load and unload than the Colt. When a latch in front of the hammer was released, the Smith & Wesson barrel and cylinder pivoted forward, automatically ejecting empties and exposing all six chambers for reloading. To reload the Colt, each individual chamber had to be aligned with a barrel-mounted ejector rod, and the single empty brass case punched out and replaced with a fresh cartridge before rotating the cylinder to the next chamber, repeating the operation a total of six times to fully load the revolver. Smiths were also generally known to have an edge in accuracy, although the Colts were simpler, sturdier, and less liable to malfunction in extreme environments. A large portion of Smith & Wesson's early production went to foreign military contracts. Other revolvers of the era included the Remington 1875, similar to the Colt pattern, and the unusual but exceptionally well-made twist-open Merwin Hulbert revolvers.

In the U.S. military, by the mid-1870s the Colt Single Action Army (SAA) and the Smith & Wesson Schofield six-shot revolvers became the Army's primary sidearms for the Indian Wars era. Although the big sixguns of the Old West are those that capture the public fancy, their production quantities were significantly less than smaller frame revolvers. Smith & Wesson offered tip-up spur-triggers and top-breaks in single or double action; Colt produced a series of single-shot derringers and spur-trigger revolvers; and Remington offered spur-trigger revolvers and its famous double derringers, in addition to other designs.

The late nineteenth century saw a proliferation of small manufacturers churning out cheap, small single-action spur-trigger revolvers, sometimes derisively referred to as "Suicide Specials." Other firms such as Harrington and Richardson, Iver Johnson, and Hopkins and Allen produced millions of inexpensive but generally serviceable small top-break and solid frame double action revolvers. These companies have been referred to as the "armorers to the nation's nightstands," accurately reflecting the fact that even persons of moderate incomes could afford their products as a handy means of home and personal protection.

Birth of the Modern Revolver

Just before the turn of the twentieth century, a new type of revolver was developed, first by Colt in 1889, followed by Smith & Wesson in 1896. This revolver used a solid frame, like the SAA, but the cylinder

Three Smith & Wesson .44 Magnums and a .38 Special hammerless Centennial engraved by Ben Shostle.

Introduction

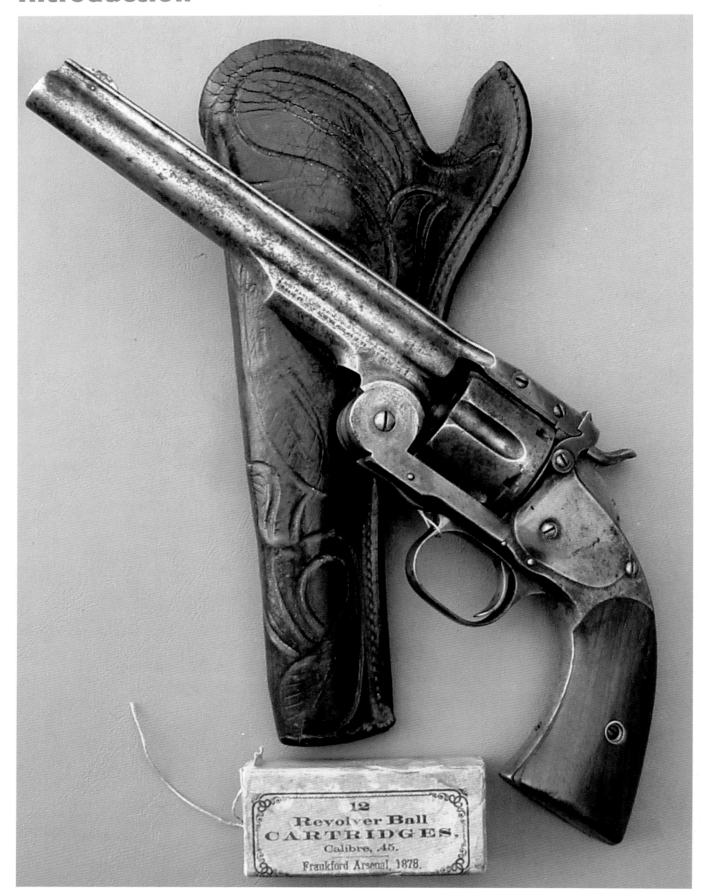

The Smith & Wesson Schofield revolver was made from 1875 to 1878 primarily for the U.S. Army where it saw service in the Indian Wars. It was also popular with lawmen and outlaws, such as this s/n 273, which is attributed to Jesse James.

swung to the side to load and unload. Empty cases were simultaneously ejected by pushing a plungerlike ejector rod at the front of the open cylinder. Smith & Wesson called their versions "Hand Ejectors" (HE) to differentiate the method of operation from their top-break automatic ejecting products.

These swing-out cylinder revolvers were also "double action" (DA), a term describing the ways in which the gun could be fired. Early revolvers were usually "single action"—the hammer had to be manually cocked before the trigger pull performed the single action of dropping the hammer to fire the round. On the DA revolvers, the gun could be fired in the traditional single action (SA) mode. Alternatively, the DA could be fired by a longer, heavier pull on the trigger, beginning with the hammer in the down,

uncocked position. In this mode, the trigger would perform the double action of first cocking and then dropping the hammer to fire the weapon. This type of revolver rapidly caught on, and would become the dominant handgun design for most of the twentieth century in America.

In its early revolvers of this type, Colt offered revolver frame sizes from its massive New Service, through handy compact pocket-sized revolvers with short 2-inch "snub nose" barrels. When the New York City police got a brash new young commissioner just before the close of the nineteenth century, he selected the little .32 Colt New Police as that department's first standard issue handgun. He also instituted the first formal police marksmanship training under the guidance of Sergeant William Petty, who happened to be a national shooting champion. The commissioner's name was Theodore Roosevelt, and a few years later he carried another swingout cylinder Colt, a New Army model, when he led the First Volunteer Cavalry up San Juan Hill in 1898.

The early Smith & Wesson HEs ranged from the large N-frame, the first of which was the famous Triple-Lock, which introduced the .44 Special cartridge, through the tiny .22 Ladysmith, which was far smaller than any swingout revolver being made today.

Smith & Wesson found the workhorse of their product line in 1899 when it made its first medium-sized K-frame "Military & Police" (M&P) revolver, chambered for their new .38 Special cartridge. Although Colt and Smith & Wesson shared the police market in the first half of the century, after World War II through the 1970s the Smith & Wesson K-frame in .38 Special was probably carried by a majority of law enforcement officers in America

The same cartridge was also popular in the smaller short-barrel five-shot J-frame "Chief's Special," serving both the police backup gun and the civilian concealed-carry market. Colt's competing Detective Special packed six rounds in a package that was only slightly larger. The little J-frame was also the platform for Smith & Wesson's "Kit Gun," a handy .22 revolver that would easily fit in a hunter's, camper's, or fisherman's kit.

Continuing through today, the .38 Special in a well-made double action revolver such as those by Smith & Wesson, Ruger, Colt, or Taurus is considered by many to be the best choice for a first-time shooter's home defense handgun. The small J-frame size is also the first choice of many experienced shooters for their personal concealed carry. The combination of safety, reliability, simplicity, and effectiveness in a gun that is small enough to carry easily, yet large enough to be manageable, is still hard to beat.

The double action system for revolvers had caught on faster in Europe than in the United States. In was used for early pinfires, and for military handguns such as Britain's ugly but reliable Webley top-breaks in .455 caliber. In 1885 smokeless powder was invented, and would lead to dramatic changes in firearms and ammunition design.

Early Auto-Loaders

A firearms design trend in Europe given a boost by the introduction of smokeless powder was the attempt to make automatic loading firearms. In general, gun designs to this point had relied on some mechanical action by the shooter to load a fresh cartridge into the

At the dawn of the twentieth century, the semiautomatic pistol design rapidly evolved, with much of the progress due to the design genius of John Moses Browning. Early Browning designed Colt auto-pistols (top to bottom): Model 1900 Sight Safey; Model 1902 Military; Model 1902 Sporting; and Model 1903 Pocket.

Introduction

The Luger represented a design advance in auto-pistols, and served as a military sidearm for Germany and other countries in the first half of the twentieth century. Shown here are scarce long-barreled variations.

firing chamber after the initial round had been fired, whether it was swiveling a lever; lifting, pulling, and pushing a bolt; or cocking the hammer or pulling the trigger to advance a revolver cylinder to the next chamber. Inventors sought a method whereby the loading of the next round would be accomplished automatically.

The first auto-loading pistol designs to see limited production were the German-made Schoenberger and Borchardt designs in 1893 and 1894 respectively. A couple years later, in 1896, the Mauser firm began manufacture of the first auto pistol to gain widespread acceptance, the Model 1896, nicknamed the Broomhandle for its slender oval cross-sectioned grip.

Germany continued its dominance in European firearms design when Georg Luger introduced his classic pistol in 1900. Whereas early automatics had used fixed box magazines, the Luger magazine mounted in the pistols grip frame, was quickly detachable and easily replaced with a fresh magazine for a quick reload. Originally manufactured in 7.63 mm (.30 cal.), in 1909 it was adapted to a new, larger diameter cartridge, and the 9 mm Luger (or 9 mm Parabellum) round was destined to become possibly the most widely used centerfire pistol ammunition of the twentieth century. The Luger was widely adopted as a military pistol by many countries, including Germany where it was designated the "Pistole 09" (P-09) for the year it was first purchased, where it served through both world wars. Its distinctive profile is widely recognized, and may be identified as "graceful" or "sinister," depending on the eye of the beholder.

(Top): Prudhomme engraved Walther Model OSP target pistol. (Bottom): Griebolt engraved Colt Police Positive.

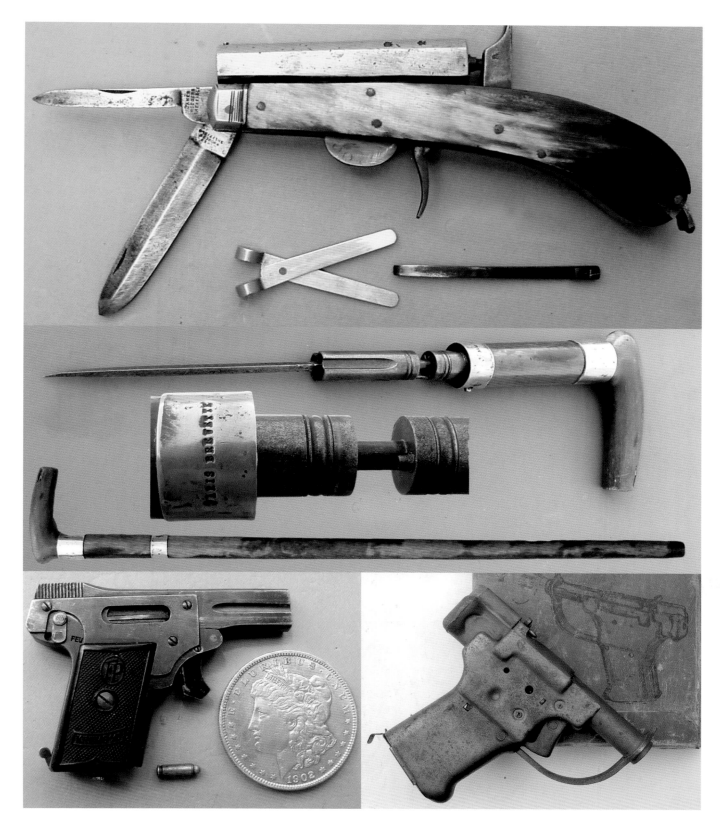

Firearms history is replete with odd and unusual designs. From top: Unwin knife pistol, ca. 1860s; cane pistol with bayonet, ca. mid-nineteenth century; tiny 2.7mm Kolibri auto-pistol, shown with silver dollar for scale, early twentieth century; U.S. military WWII "Liberator" single shot sheet metal .45 acp pistol, designed to be dropped to partisan forces behind enemy lines and intended as a "use a gun to get a gun" one-use weapon to kill an enemy soldier to acquire his more-effective weapon.

John Moses Browning

At this point in the history of firearms, we must travel back across the Atlantic, and back a few years in time to track the career of probably the greatest firearms inventor of all time, John Moses Browning of Ogden, Utah. Browning was a prolific inventor and innovator, and his designs for lever-action rifles, single-shot rifles, and shotguns are still being produced today.

It was in the area of automatic firearms, however, that Browning possibly made his greatest advances. Auto-loaders use the part of the force of the firing cartridge to eject the empty casing and load a fresh round into the chamber. This may occur by direct or delayed blowback of the breechblock, by utilizing the recoil of the gun, or by redirecting some of the expanding gases of the burning gunpowder from the barrel to operate the action.

In 1900, the same year as the Luger was introduced, Colt first offered a Browning designed auto-loading pistol, the .38 caliber Model 1900 Automatic. Variations and improvements followed in rapid succession, with a smaller Hammerless .32 Pocket model in 1903, and a tiny "vest pocket" sized .25 caliber pistol in 1908. Colt introduced the .45 Automatic Colt Pistol (ACP) cartridge in the Browning designed Model 1905.

This is the cartridge that would be chambered in the famous Model 1911. The 1911 was rapidly adopted by the US military, and, only slightly modified over time, remained the primary US issue sidearm through out the Vietnam War. Colt and many other firms continue production of 1911 pattern pistols today, and they still serve military, law enforcement, and personal protection duty on a regular basis. It is the handgun of choice for many shooting sports that seek to simulate combat-type shooting, and in accurized forms is dominant in many traditional target shooting sports. Its mastery requires effort, training, and practice, but in the right hands, many would argue that it is the finest combat handgun of all time.

Introduction

The Model 1911 pattern semiauto pistol is widely considered to be one of the finest fighting handguns ever made, and has served with military and law enforcement for nearly a century.

While the 1911 may have been Browning's finest handgun design, his contributions did not end there. His final pistol design, the Model 1935, took advantage of the Luger's smaller diameter 9 mm cartridge "double stacked" in two parallel columns in the detachable magazine for a total magazine capacity of thirteen rounds (compared to seven rounds in a 1911 mag). The 1935 is also known as the Browning High Power.

It's worth mentioning that most detachable magazine auto-loading pistols present a potential hazard for untrained individuals. It's easy to check whether most double action revolvers are loaded simply by swinging open the cylinder and looking. However, a person who is not familiar with firearms may assume that an auto-loading firearm is unloaded once the magazine has been removed. This is a potentially lethal mistake. An auto-loading pistol may still have a live round in the chamber after the magazine has been taken out. In most designs, this round will fire if the trigger is pulled, with the potential for tragic consequences.

Modern Gun Milestones

Recent decades have witnessed the continuing evolution and development of other types of sporting firearms, with several recurring trends.

Handguns, and revolvers in particular, have seen the development of more and more powerful ammunition. In 1935 Smith & Wesson rocked the handgun world with the introduction of the .357 Magnum cartridge and their prestigious Registered Magnum revolver to fire it. At a time when full power "big bore" handgun rounds ran in the 300 to 350 ft/lb muzzle energy range, Smith & Wesson upped the ante to over 500 ft/lbs Results of actual law enforcement shootings suggest that the .357 Magnum round, with 125 grain hollowpoint loads, may be the most effective "stopper" still today. The fact that revolvers chambered for the .357 Magnum can also shoot the milder .38 Special has contributed to their continuing popularity.

Smith & Wesson followed this with the .44 Magnum in 1955. With muzzle energy approaching 1,000 ft/lbs., the .44 Magnum changed handgun big game hunting

Colt military handguns include the Model 1911A1 in .45 ACP; the General Officers Pistol in .32 ACP or .380 ACP; and the .38 Special Commando model.

from a "stunt" to a serious and common sporting pursuit. When the movies hit the theaters, lots of folks with more imagination than experience decided they needed "the world's most powerful handgun," not understanding how to manage the considerable recoil. It was not uncommon to find a Smith & Wesson .44 Magnum advertised for sale in "as new" condition,

with six cartridges missing from the fifty round-box. Once around the cylinder was enough for many would-be Harry Callahans!

Just recently, Smith & Wesson raised the bar to a previously unimaginable level with the introduction of their X-frame .500 Magnum revolver. Developing an incredible 2,500 ft/lbs of muzzle energy, the 500

A World War II 1911A1 pistol believed to have been the first one carried by a U.S. serviceman onto the main island of Japan, and a compact model attributed to a Texas ranger.

Top to bottom: Weldon Bledsoe engraved Smith & Wesson Model 25, .45 ACP revolver; Ben Shostle engraved Luger 9 mm; Cole Agee engraved Colt Detective Special .38.

readily surpasses the power level of many high power rifles.

Auto-pistol evolution took a leap forward in 1971 when the Smith & Wesson Model 59 was the first to combine the Browning High Power high capacity double stack magazine with the double action mechanism of the German World War II–era Walther P-38. A number of firms followed suit, and the genre, known as "wonder nines" for their usual 9 mm chambering, began to make inroads into a police market that previously had been dominated by double action revolvers. The Swiss-based firm of Sig Sauer developed a strong reputation for quality and reliability in this type of pistol, and the Beretta Model 92 in the wonder nine configuration replaced the old warhorse 1911A1 pistol as the U.S. Army standard issue.

In 1982 the semiautomatic pistol market was turned upside down by a new Austrian manufacturer offering a radically different design with the frame made from plasticlike polymer. Traditionalists initially scoffed at the seventeen-round design with no external manual safeties other than a lever on the face of trigger, and an operating system that was neither SA nor DA, but instead called a "safe action" by the maker. Tupperware jokes abounded. At the other end of the spectrum, anti-gun fanatics ranted and frothed at the mouth over "plastic guns" that would be "invisible" to airport X-ray machines (not true).

However, beauty is as beauty does, and the Glock did nothing but perform, combining reliability, simplicity, affordability, and functional accuracy. Today, it is likely that more Glocks ride in police holsters than any other make.

The trend to new materials other than traditional blue steel and wood had begun years before. Smith & Wesson used lightweight alloys to make lightweight guns easier to carry, beginning with aluminum frame

Airweight Chiefs Specials in 1952 and continuing through scandium and titanium alloys today that get .38 revolver weights down to the ten-ounce range.

Smith & Wesson and Charter Arms led the way in using rust-resistant stainless steel for small revolvers likely to be carried in sweaty environments close to the body, beginning in the mid-1960s. Since then, stainless steel has nearly replaced blue carbon steel in revolver designs, and has made major inroads in long gun and semi-auto pistol production.

Many major handgun makers have followed Glock's lead in offering synthetic framed auto-pistols, and synthetic stock have been found to be more lightweight and less affected by environmental extremes than wood for long gun stocks. Rubber has replaced wood as the most likely handgun grip material.

Probably the last of the great firearms inventors in the tradition of Sam Colt and D. B. Wesson was Bill Ruger. His Sturm, Ruger firm developed a reputation for improving classic sporting gun designs, and turning out a broad line of well-made and reasonably priced firearms, from revolvers and rifles through auto-pistols and over-under shotguns.

Other new firms sprang up to challenge the old line makers with improved or cheaper versions of the classic designs. Springfield Armory has become a major maker of military pattern sporting arms based on classic military designs such as the 1911 pistol. Taurus began to offer serious competition to Smith & Wesson in the revolver field. Other makers such as Uberti and Navy Arms saw the strong nostalgia market for ninteenth-century designs, and began to produce quality version of early percussion revolvers, Single Action Armies, and other arms appealing to Old West buffs and participants in the fun new sport of cowboy action shooting.

Options for aiming a firearm have expanded dramatically over the past fifty years. Telescopic sights for precision rifle shooting were used as early as the Civil War. However, it wasn't until after World War II that it became a standard practice to mount a scope on serious hunting rifles, and the technology of these optics has continually evolved and improved. In the 1970s and 1980s, scopes came to be used on hunting handguns. New forms of sighting equipment, such as electronic red dot sights, glow in the dark night sights, and ultra-compact laser aiming systems, and even night vision scopes, have come on the market and met with acceptance.

Enjoying Firearms

Firearms ownership and usage is a treasured American tradition. There are two fundamental requirements for those who would participate in this experience.

The first is of course safety. Everyone needs to know the basic safety rules by heart. There are many, but the following, if committed to memory and followed religiously, will prevent tragic mishaps:

1. Treat every firearm as if it is loaded.
2. Never let the muzzle point at anything you are not willing to see destroyed.
3. Do not touch the trigger until your sights are on target.
4. Be sure of your target, and what is beyond it. Firearms projectiles can travel long distances, and will penetrate many visual barriers.
5. Keep your firearms so they are not accessible to unauthorized, untrained, or irresponsible individuals.

Even folks who choose not to own guns need to be sure their children understand basic gun safety. For the smallest kids, the National Rifle Association (NRA's) Eddy Eagle program has a basic, easy to remember drill for what they should do if they come across a gun:

1. Stop!
2. Don't touch.
3. Leave the area.
4. Tell an adult.

No one is born knowing how to shoot. If you choose to own a firearm, get instruction in how to use it safely and effectively. Even if you don't own a gun, such training can still be a good idea, as it may someday be as vital to you or a loved one as is training in CPR.

The NRA is the largest firearms training organization in the world, and offers solid programs for folks from beginning to advanced shooters. Ask a local gun shop, gun club, shooting range, or police department to put you in touch with an NRA certified program.

This brings us to the second requirement for firearms owner: vigilance.

There is a special genius to the Bill of Rights of the U.S. Constitution, which protects the individual and collective civil rights of Americans. It is no mistake that the second amendment to that document provides that ". . . the right of the people to keep and bear arms shall not be infringed."

If it were not for the National Rifle Association, that basic human right would have been lost long ago. It's an ongoing battle; not always an easy or popular one, but an essential one nonetheless.

Classic large caliber double barreled Howdah pistol was the prefered weapon of army officers detached to the wildest territories of the British Empire during the nineteenth century.

ArmaLite

ArmaLite was founded in Hollywood, California, in 1954 as a division of Fairchild Engine and Airlane Corporation. The company was set up mainly by Fairchild employee, George Sullivan.

For more than half a century, there had been little development in small arms—most of the interest and changes were with the semiautomatic rifles and machine guns. The AR-5 .22 Hornet Survival Rifle was ArmaLite's first major new product. The U.S. Air Force soon adopted the AR-5 as the MA-1 Survival Rifle.

Through the remainder of the 1950s, ArmaLite focused on the development and manufacture of military firearms and the creation of modern lightweight weapons employing newly developed plastics and alloys.

In 1961 Fairchild was having financial difficulties and the principals of the ArmaLite division were able to purchase the company. ArmaLite switched its emphasis and embarked on a new phase in the company's growth, as ArmaLite Incorporated.

In 1983 ArmaLite was sold to Elisco Tool Manufacturing Company in the Philippines. Independent of ArmaLite, Karl Lewis and Jim Glazier formed a company named Eagle Arms in Coal Valley Illinois in 1986. In January 1994, Mr. Mark Westrom purchased the company. John Ugarte had retained rights to the ArmaLite trademark. In early 1995, Westrom purchasedthose rights, and production of ArmaLite rifles resumed in Illinois. The corporation wasreorganized as ArmaLite, with Eagle Arms converted to a division of ArmaLite. First shipments of new ArmaLite rifles began in 1995.

AR24K-13C

AR24-13 Custom

AR24-15

AR24-13 Compact

AR24-15 Custom

Baikal

Baikal—Federal State Unitary Plant "IZHEVSKY MEKHANICHESKY ZAVOD" (FSUP "IMZ")—is one of the largest businesses within the Russian Agency on Conventional Armament.

In 1944 the first production facility went into operation, producing motorcycles, mining equipment, and scales.

From 1945 to 1955, the company produced more than 5 million of the new army Makarov pistols, one of the best of its kind. Also during this period, in 1949, the company began the manufacture of the ZK simple single-barrel model and the IZH-49 double-barrel gun. The Baikal plant became one of the largest manufacturers of sporting and hunting guns in the world.

An important hallmark not only for the company but also for firearms manufacturing in general was the 1956 opening of the Gunsmithing and Engraving School to train qualified gun makers.

The intervening decades were devoted to the production of a wide range of firearms and other products for the Soviet military. The number of government orders greatly decreased by 1990, and Baikal turned its attention to increasing its manufacture and types of hunting, sporting, and personal firearms.

In the 1990s, Baikal for the first time was able to export products to the United States. The legendary Makarov pistol was replaced by the 9 mm Yarygin army pistol in 2000. Today Baikal firearms are available in more than sixty-five countries.

Yarygin Pistol

Makarov Pistol

PSM

442

MP-71H

Baikal

MP-75

MP-79

MP-81

26

Margo

MP-446 "Viking"

MP-446C "Viking"

MP-461 "STRAZHNIK"

Beretta

Founded in 1526, Beretta is one of the oldest corporations in the world. For almost 500 years, Beretta has been owned by the same family. The earliest bill of sale in the company archives indicates that in 1526, gunsmith Maestro Bartolomeo Beretta of Gardone Val Trompia (Brescia, Lombardy, Italy) sold 185 arquebus (heavy musket needing to be propped up by supports) barrels to the Arsenal of Venice. Over the span of nearly five centuries, Beretta developed from a small guild operation making exquisitely detailed and precision-handmade firearms to an international firm trading in more than 100 countries and using the most modern forms of manufacture, including robotics.

By the twentieth century, the company was producing both military and sporting firearms. This marked the onset of decades of incredible growth. At the end of the nineteenth century, Beretta had 130 employees and a single 10,000-square-foot factory. By 2000, its factories took up more than 75,000 square feet of space in Gardone and another 50,000 square feet at sites in Italy, Spain, and the United States (Maryland).

During World War II, Beretta manufactured rifles and pistols for the Italian military until the 1943 Armistice between Italy and the Allied forces. The Germans still controlled the northern part of Italy,

and they seized the Beretta factories and continued producing arms until 1945.

In the 1950s, Beretta expanded into automobile and motorcycle production. A true indication of its international fame came in the 1960s, however, when Ian Fleming's master spy, James Bond 007, carried a 25-caliber Beretta in both books and film.

Today, the company is owned and is run by Ugo Gussalli Beretta (a direct descendant of Bartolomeo) and his sons, Franco and Pietro. One of the world's great arms producers, Beretta makes more than 1,500 pieces each day, ranging from portable firearms (shotguns for hunting and competition, pump-action guns, semiautomatic pistols, and assault rifles). Although more than 90 percent of their production is in sporting firearms, Beretta also supplies arms to the Italian military, the U.S. Armed Forces and State Police, France's Gendarmerie Nationale and the French Air Force, the Spanish Guardia Civil, and the Turkish Police Force, among others.

The parent company, Beretta Holding, controls Beretta USA, Benelli, Franchi, SAKO, Stoeger, Tikka, Uberti, the Burris Optics Company, and 20 percent interest of the Browning arms company.

Nano

92A1

21 Bobcat

Cheetah

Target

3032 Tomcat 32

92FS

Cougar Inox

Beretta

9000 S Type

M9 A1

M9 05

Px4 Sub

Px4

Px4 Compact

Px4 Sub with X2 Laser

Px4 Storm Inox

Beretta

U22 Neos 4.5

U22 Neos 4.5 Inox

92FS Vertec with M6 Laser

Stampede 4.75"

Stampede Inox

Stampede Marshall

Browning

The Browning Arms Company opened in Ogden, Utah, in 1927, one year after the death of John Moses Browning, the renowned gunsmith and firearms inventor from whom the company took its name. In 1852 Jonathon Browning, father of John, had set up his first gun store in Ogden. After Jonathon's death in 1872, John Moses Browning and his five brothers established Browning Brothers Company, a retail arms business. John Browning is known as the greatest firearms inventor in history.

Browning had 128 gun patents; during his years as an inventor more than 50 million guns were produced from those patents. His best known, and most widely sold guns, included the 45-caliber pistol, the 1895 Colt Peacemaker machine gun, the Browning automatic rifle, several 30- and 50-caliber machine guns, and the Browning Automatic-5 shotgun, which was first made in 1902 and is manufactured still today. The Browning Company also became well known for other products such as gun safes, knives, and shooting and hunting apparel.

The actual production of the guns eventually was handed over to a number of firearm manufacturers, including Winchester Arms, the Colt Arms Manufacturing Company, and the Fabrique Nationale of Belgium, the Remington Arms Company, and Savage Arms Company. All of these produce guns from John Browning's patents.

The Fabrique Nationale of Belgium purchased the company in 1977, but the world headquarters is still located just outside of Ogden, Utah, in Mountain Green. By 1989 the sales for the company exceeded $100 million just in the United States. Today Browning's company catalog includes sporting rifles and guns, knives, pistols, fishing gear, outdoor clothing, and golf clubs.

Hi-Power MkIII

Hi-Power Std.

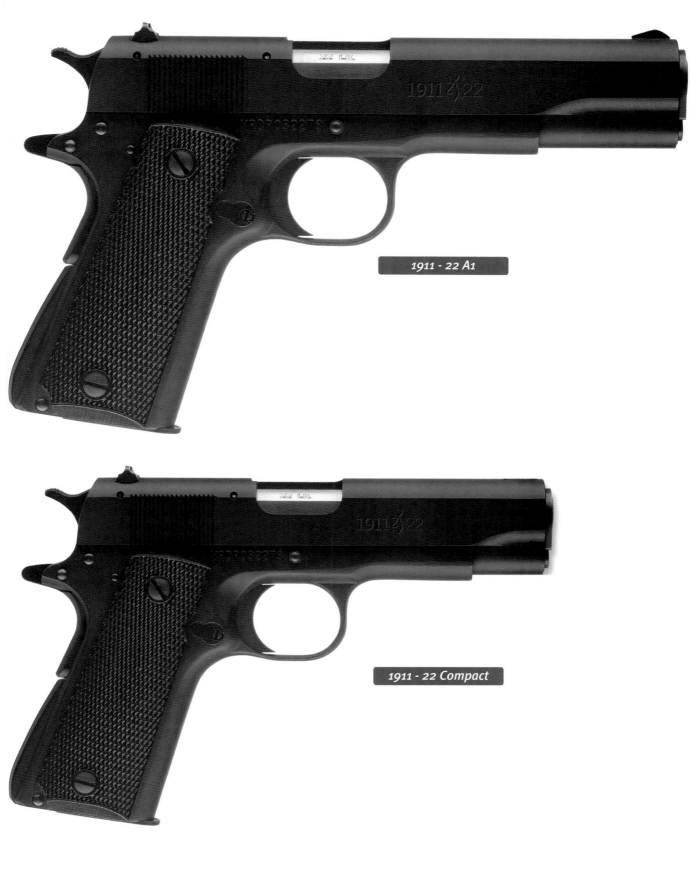

1911 - 22 A1

1911 - 22 Compact

PRO - 9

Buck Mark Camper

Buck Mark Camper Stainless

Buck Mark Challenge

MKIII Digital Green

Buck Mark 5.5 Field

Buck Mark 5.5 Target

Buck Mark Hunter

Buck Mark Micro Std. URX

Buck Mark Std. Stainless URX

Buck Mark Bullseye Target URX

Buck Mark Lite Splash 7.25 URX

Buck Mark Contour 7.25 URX

Buck Mark Bullseye Target Stainless

*Buck Mark Plus Stainless
Black Laminated UDX*

*Full Line Dealer Buck Mark
Plus Rosewood UDX*

Cased 1911-22 Commemorative with Knife

Charter Arms

In 1964, wanting to produce reliable yet affordable handguns, firearms designer Douglas McClenahan started Charter Arms along the Connecticut River in New England, often known as Gun Valley, where the first firearms in the United States were developed and manufactured. He had learned his trade working for Colt, High Standard, and Sturm, Ruger.

"The Undercover," a .38 Special five-shot revolver, was the first pistol developed and produced by the new company. This pistol was a new innovation on the older models with side plate specifications other arms makers put on a one-piece frame. The new gun had much greater strength and could safely shoot hot loads. The gun also had fewer moving parts, and McClenahan devised a safety feature, a unique hammer block system, for the firing device.

Charter Arms became known as a producer of inexpensive yet quality handguns. The best known of their famous revolvers were the .44 Special Bulldog and .38 Special Bulldog Pug.

In the 1990s, one of the original investors, David Eckert, bought out the firm. The company continued to produce the successful Charter Arms firearms with some new modifications, including a one-piece barrel and front sight, as well as an improved safety blocked hammer innovation.

In 2008 Charter Arms introduced a new line of Patriot revolvers, chambered for the .327 Federal Magnum, and a new revolver: the Charter Arms Rimless Revolver.

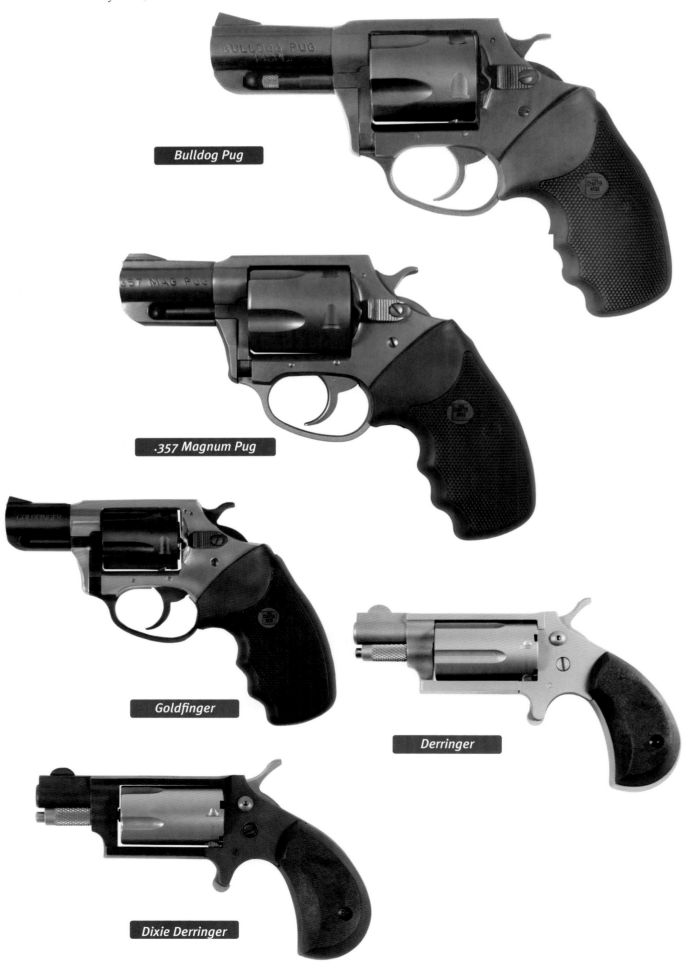

Bulldog Pug

.357 Magnum Pug

Goldfinger

Derringer

Dixie Derringer

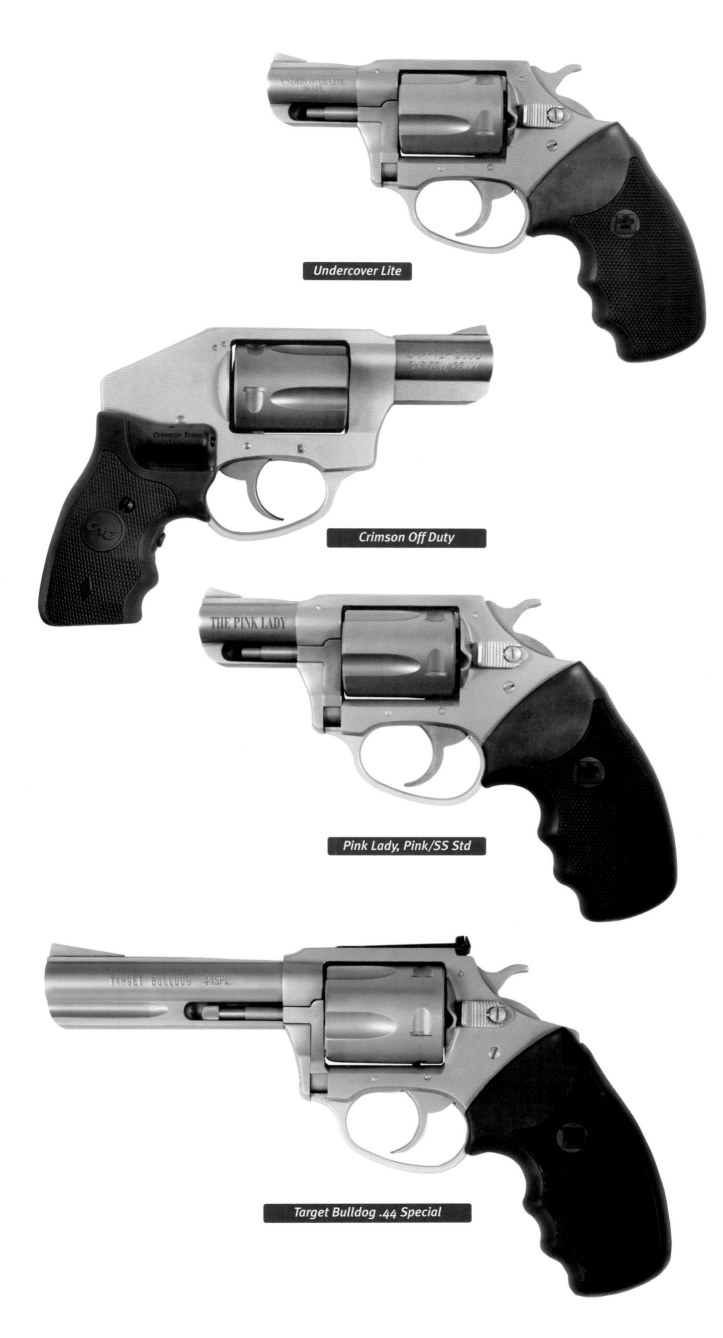

Undercover Lite

Crimson Off Duty

Pink Lady, Pink/SS Std

Target Bulldog .44 Special

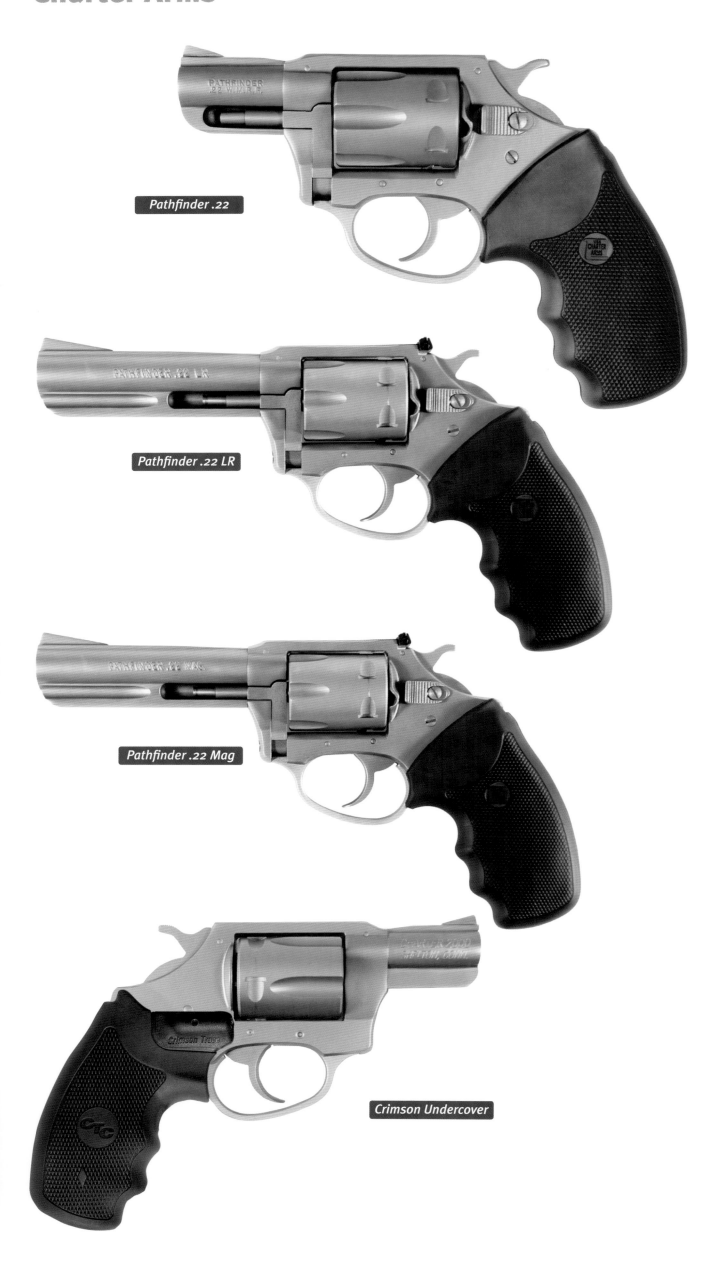

Pathfinder .22

Pathfinder .22 LR

Pathfinder .22 Mag

Crimson Undercover

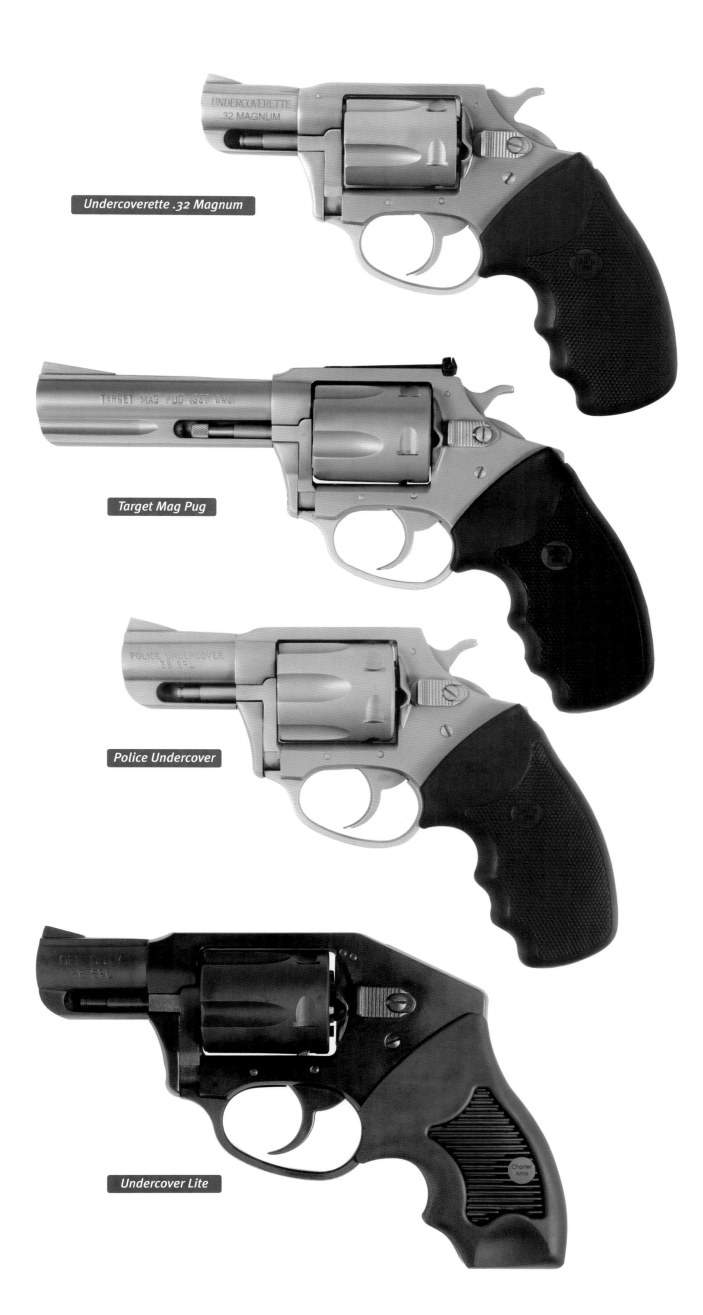

Undercoverette .32 Magnum

Target Mag Pug

Police Undercover

Undercover Lite

Colt

Founded in Hartford, Connecticut, in 1847, Colt's Manufacturing Company (CMC, formerly Colt's Patent Firearms Manufacturing Company) is a U.S. firearms manufacturer famous for the development and production of a wide range of firearms including military and civilian arms.

The fame of the company was built on the patent held by Samuel Colt, who designed and produced the first working revolver, the Colt .45 or Single Action Army or Peacemaker. This handgun would revolutionize the firearm world with its revolving cylinder that could hold five or six bullets. The gun was the most used firearm in the American West in the nineteenth century.

The preeminence of Colt in the firearms business of the latter half of the nineteenth century is evident in the post–Civil War slogan: "Abe Lincoln may have freed all men, but Sam Colt made them equal." The Colt revolvers were often referred to as "the Great Equalizers" since they could be loaded and fired by almost anyone. It became the best known firearm not only in North America but also in many European countries.

Although the M16 was not developed by Colt, they were for a long time responsible for its production along with other related firearms. Throughout the twentieth century, Colt continued to manufacture an innovative line of firearms.

In 2002 Colt Manufacturing Company split off a separate division—Colt Defense—to manufacture firearm lines exclusively for the military, law enforcement agencies, and private security firms around the world. Now Colt Manufacturing Company produces firearms and accessories solely for the civilian market of hunters, sports enthusiasts, and for home security.

Gold Cup

MK IV

1991

Mustang Pocketlite

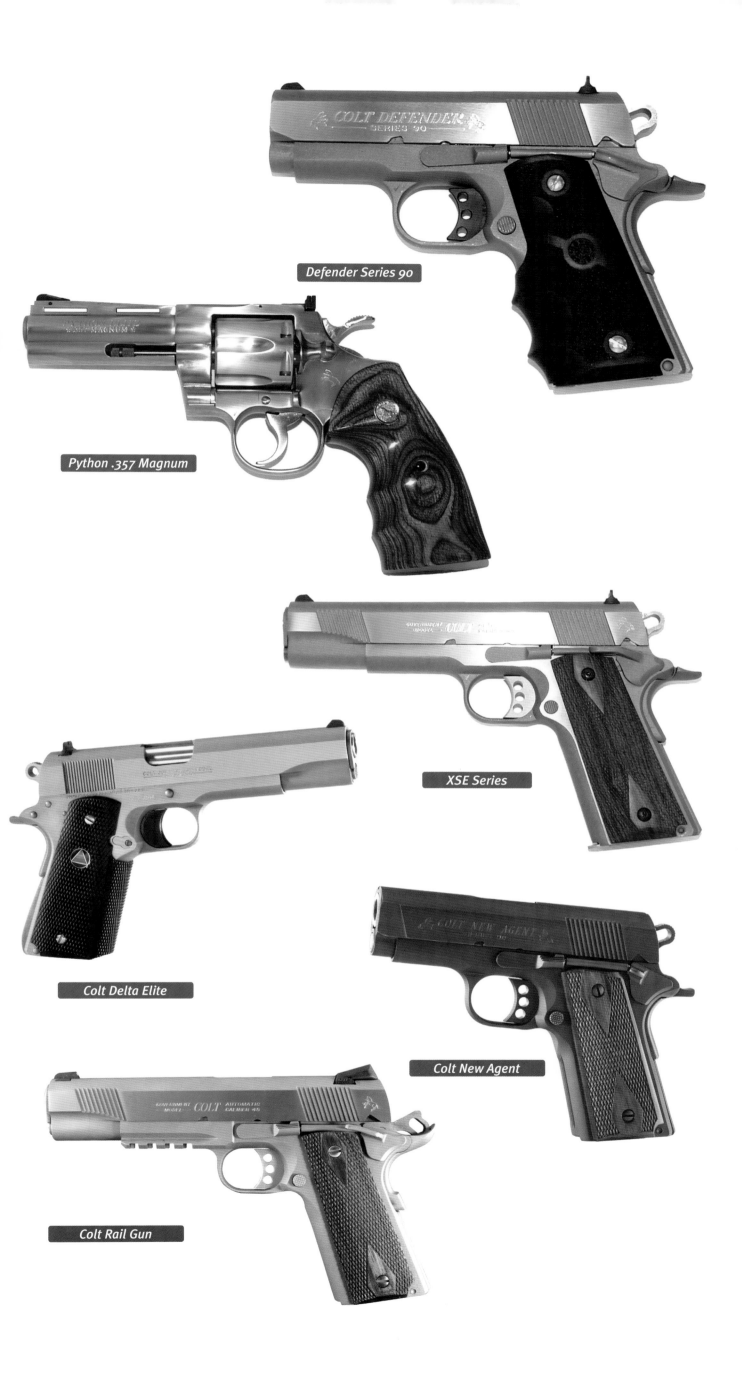

Defender Series 90

Python .357 Magnum

XSE Series

Colt Delta Elite

Colt New Agent

Colt Rail Gun

CZUB

The beginnings of Ceska zbrojovka Uhersky Brod (CZUB) were in 1936, when it was established as a division of Ceska zbrojovka in the town of Uhersky Brod in Czechoslovakia, now in the Czech Republic. The first firearms produced by the fledgling company were machine guns for aircraft, military pistols and small bore rifles. During the years of Nazi Occupation during World War II, the workers at the plant were made to produce and repairs weapons for the Germans. After the war, beginning in 1945, CZUB manufactured both military and civilian firearms

In 1950, the company became a totally separate government enterprise, "Presne strojirenstvi Uhersky Brod" (The Precision Machine Tooling Company), and was set up with a number of specialized subdivisions. During the decades of the Cold War, CZUB produced a range of military armaments including both rifles and pistols. Through the 1970s and 1980s, the firm was merged with other companies and worked in producing airplane engines and tractors. .

By the 1990s, the company was once more an independent entity devoted to producing a range of firearms and reassuming the name eská zbrojovka, s.p. In 1992, the joint stock company Ceska zbrojovka a.s., Uhersky Brod was established in agreement with a Czech privatization project and the decentralization of government concerns. As it joined the economy of the free world, CZUB sold weapons in more than 60 countries. In 1997, it opened CZ-USA in the United States and continues to produce military, law enforcement and recreational firearms. Today, CZUB has more than 2000 employees and is one of the world's largest arms manufacturers.

75 Compact

75B Stainless

Czechmate LTD

75 SP-01

75 Tactical Sport

75 SP-01 Phantom

Shadow Custom 2tone

83 Stainless

85 Combat

97 Tactical

CZ75 P07

100B

2075 Rami P

09 Skorpion

Dan Wesson

In 1968 Daniel B. Wesson—great-grandson and namesake of the legendary D. B. Wesson who confounded Smith & Wesson in 1852—established his own firearms company, Dan Wesson. His goal was to create superb, nearly indestructible firearms, each of which would bear his name. The slogan of the company was "the Innovator'" and that was Wesson's goal: to create innovative top quality guns.

The product line of the company included the model 12, .357 magnum, a large-frame 44 magnum line, and the massive Super Mag. In 1996 Robert Seva purchased Dan Wesson and moved the manufacturing firm from Massachusetts to Norwich, New York. Seva started on the production of a line of revolvers, although few were produced during the first years. Production went slowly as the company strove to maintain the standards of excellence that were synonymous with a Dan Wesson firearm.

They expanded the product line to include a 1911-style pistol, again designed and produced to rigorous standards. In 2005, CZ-USA acquired Dan Wesson, eager to add the company's line of revolvers and reputation for innovation and quality.

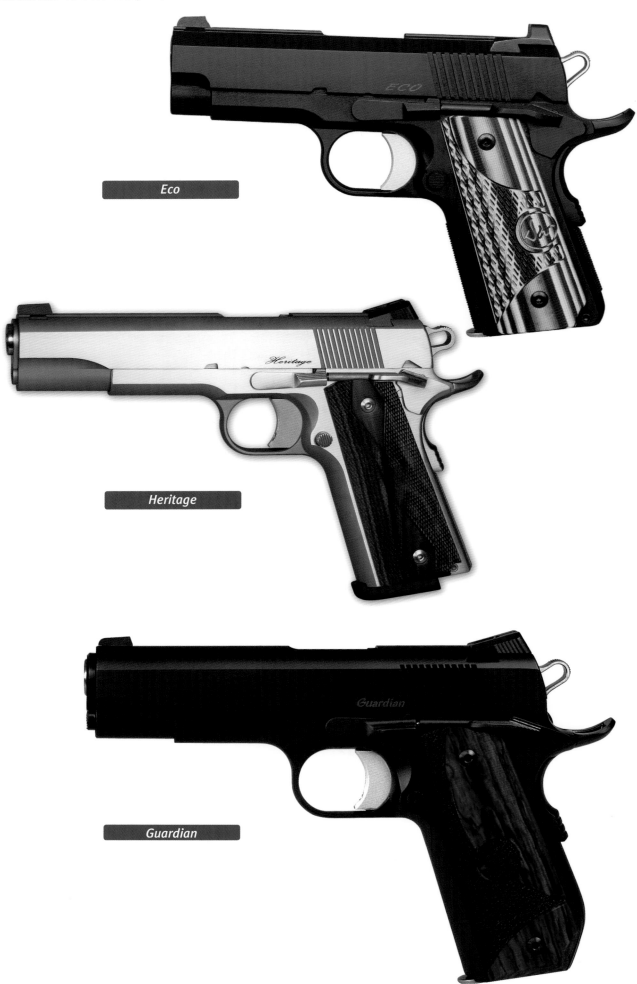

Eco

Heritage

Guardian

Titan

RZ-10

Specialist

7445 Safari VH8

Dan Wesson

V-Bob

Valor

CCO Bobtail

715 .357 Magnum

Havoc

Pointman 7-40

Pointman 9

Elite Series Mayhem

FNH

FNH, formally known as Fabrique Nationale Herstal, was founded in 1889 in the small town of Herstal outside of Liege in Belgium. Today "FN" is a subsidiary of the Herstal Group, which also owns U.S. Repeating Arms Company (Winchester) and Browning Arms Company.

In 1889 the company joined other arms manufacturers as a part of a company named Fabrique Nationale d'Armes de Guerre (FN) to help produce 150,000 Mauser Model 89 rifles ordered by the Belgian government.

In 1897 the company acquired the license for John Browning's 7.65 Browning pistol with its innovative locking system. This was the beginning of a long and productive collaboration between the Belgian company FN and Browning, the Utah inventor. In fact, Browning's son, Val, carries on his father's work with the company.

In the beginning of the twentieth century, FN also became involved in producing cars, motorcycles, and trucks. In 1914 the two bullets that killed the Archduke Ferdinand and set off World War I came from an FN Model 1910 semiautomatic pistol in 7.65 x 17 mm (.32 ACP).

In the 1930s, Browning designed his renowned .50 Cal M2 machine gun which is still manufactured by FN today.

In the later part of the twentieth century, FN helped to develop and produce both machine guns and light rifles used by NATO forces. Through to the present day, FN has continued to develop and produce innovative firearms and weapons systems that are deployed by the military by land, sea, and air.

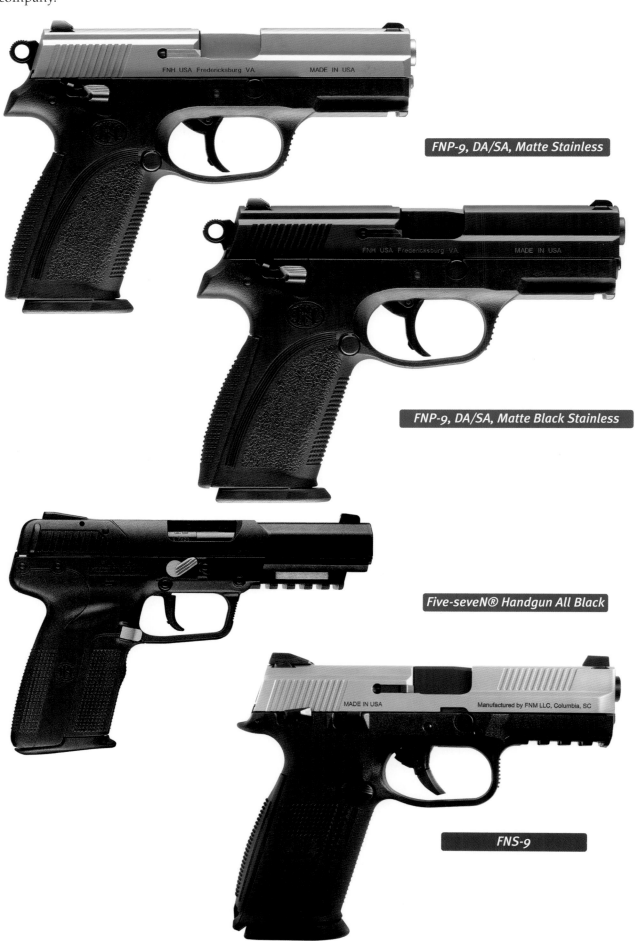

FNP-9, DA/SA, Matte Stainless

FNP-9, DA/SA, Matte Black Stainless

Five-seveN® Handgun All Black

FNS-9

FNP-9M, DA/SA, Matte Black Stainless

FNP-45, DA/SA, USG

FNP-40, DA/SA, Matte Black Stainless

FNX-40

FNP-40, DA/SA, Matte Stainless

FNP-45, DA/SA, Matte Black Stainless

FNP-45, DA/SA, Matte Stainless

FNP-40, DA/SA, USG

FNP-9, DA/SA, USG

357 Matte Silver Stainless

Glock

In 1963 Gaston Glock founded Glock GmbH (trademarked as GLOCK) with headquarters in Deutsch-Wagram, Austria, not far from Vienna. At first, the company produced plastic curtain rods, later adding lines of plastic boxes, shovels, utility knives, and machine gun ammo belts. It was not until the early 1980s that Glock produced its first firearm, the Glock 17, a 9 mm Luger Parabellum handgun with a capacity of seventeen rounds. The Austrian army eventually selected this pistol as their weapon of choice. In 1984 Glock went international, selling the Glock 17 to the Norwegian army.

Most known for the production of polymer-framed pistols, it also manufactures field knives and entrenching tools.

The majority of U.S. law enforcement agencies and the military personnel today carry Glocks. They are often the weapon of choice by civilians for personal protection and competitive shooting. The Multi-

National Forces in Iraq as well as the Iraqi military and Iraqi National Police are armed with Glock handguns. The continuing popularity of Glock's line of handguns is due to its reliability in extreme conditions, small number of parts that makes maintenance easier, and its use of a wide range of ammunition. Because of the polymer plastic framework, the guns are relatively light.

The high profile and strong selling history of Glock pistols motivated several firearm manufacturers to begin production of similar polymer-framed firearms. These include the Springfield Armory XD, Steyr MA1, Smith & Wesson M&P, and Walther.

Glock 20

Glock 29

Glock 34

Glock 17

Glock 22

Glock

Glock 26

Glock 35

Glock 39

Glock 27

Glock 18

Glock 19

Glock 24C

Glock 31

Heckler & Koch

In 1949 three former Mauser Company engineers, Edmund Heckler, Theodor Koch, and Alex Seidel, joined together to form Heckler & Koch (H&K). In the early years, H&K made machine tools, parts for sewing machines, gauges, and other precision parts. By 1956 the firm was offering to produce the G3 automatic rifle for the Bundeswehr (German Federal Army).

Over the years since, H&K has designed and formulated more than 100 weapons creating a lightweight polymer line of assault rifles, the G36 of firearms for military and police organizations around the globe. In 1991 the company was bought by British Aerospace's Royal Ordinance division. Since then, their work in weaponry has mainly concentrated on modifying and perfecting the SA80 rifle series for the British Army and creating a line of lightweight polymer assault rifles, the G36.

In 2002, H&K was sold to a German group (H&K Beteiligungs-GmbH) that was created for the purpose of this acquisition.

Located in Oberndorf in Baden-Württemberg, H&K also has subsidiaries in the United Kingdom, France, and the United States. "Keine Kompromisse!" (No Compromise!) is the company's motto, emphasizing their desire to produce accurate reliable products with ergonomic efficiency, and not sacrificing any one for the other. Today they provide firearms to the Special Air Service, U.S. Navy SEALs, Delta Force, FBI HRT, Kentucky State Police SRT, the German KSK and GSG 9, and many other counter-terrorist and hostage rescue teams. In 2004 the U.S. Department of Homeland Security awarded a contract to H&K for delivery of up to 65,000 pistols, the largest contract in United States law enforcement history.

P30

Mark 23

P2000 SK

HK 45 Compact

P30S

HK 45 & H45C

USP .45

USP Long

USP Compact

USP .45 Tactical

USP Expert with USL

USP Expert

USP Compact .45

USP .45 Compact Tactical with suppressor

Heckler & Koch

USP Expert .45

USP Compact .357

P2000 with surefire

Hi-Point

Hi-Point Firearms established its place in the firearms market by producing polymer-framed semiautomatic pistols, selling inexpensively, and foregoing the aesthetics. Many of Hi-Point's pistols are heavy, but have few parts making them easier to maintain. Instead of the more common breech-locking system, the pistols employ a heavy slide that keeps the breech closed through its size and weight. In the field, the pistols do require a special punch or screwdriver to permit field-stripping.

The slide itself is diecast from an alloy of aluminum, magnesium, and copper known as zamak-3. Most other slides are made from forged steel. Located in Mansfield, Ohio, Hi-Point favors the diecasting

method since they are located in an area of Ohio that is home to many companies that manufacture diecast parts for automobiles, and Hi-Point has taken advantage of their presence.

Hi-Point carbines are also manufactured with a polymer stock, stamped sheet metal receiver cover, and a bolt cast from zamak-3. Steel, however, is used for the barrel of the carbine. They utilize blowback action usually most practical for a low-pressure carbine.

40 SWB

45 ACP

C-9

CF-380

Kahr Arms

Kahr Arms gun manufacturing company was established in 1992 by Justin Moon, son of Reverend Sun Myung Moon, founder of the Unification Church. The corporate headquarters are in Blauvelt, New York; the manufacturing facility is in Worcester, Massachusetts, in the heart of "Gun Valley." Moon was responsible for the design of the first firearms that Kahr produced and holds six patents for gun design.

Kahr was not a stand-alone corporation, but rather was a division of Saeilo, a company noted for its precision metalworking. Saeilo was able to offer guidance and support to the new firearms company on precision production techniques. Already in 2001, 220 Saeilo workers and more than 20 percent of Saeilo's profits came from the Kahr Arms division.

Kahr Arms's specialty is the design and production of small, concealable pistols. In 1999, however, Kahr Arm's purchased Auto-Ordnance Corporation, famous as the maker of Thompson submachine guns, the famous semiautomatic "Tommy Gun."

Since the 1990s, laws have been changed in many states allowing permits for carrying concealed weapons. The Kahr line of compact pistols has benefitted in increased sales. Kahr was one of the first companies to produce and market small, finely made pistols that could fire eight or fewer relatively large 9 mm and .40-caliber bullets. Due to single-stack magazines, the pistol was both slender and compact.

CW9

K9 Matte Stainless

CM40

K9 Matte Blackened Stainless

K9 Polished Stainless

P380

P9 Black Polymer, Stainless

*P9 Black Polymer,
Blackened Stainless*

T9 Novak

MK9 Matte Stainless

MK9 Elite

TP9 Novak

Kimber

In 1979 Greg and Jack Warne first established Kimber (originally known as "Kimber of Oregon") in Clackamas, Oregon, a suburb of Portland. The name came from Jack Warne's birthplace in Australia, Kimba-Abo (which means "bush fire"). Jack had been the head of Sporting Arms (SportCo) a premier firearms company he had started in Adelaide, Australia. In 1968 his company was bought out by Omark Industries, based in Portland, and Jack came to the United States as president of Omark.

Kimber's early reputation in the field was built on the quality of their .22-caliber long rifles patterned after the bolt-action Winchesters. Soon they needed to expand their manufacturing capabilities and so opened a second production facility in nearby Colton, Oregon. They also became renowned for their quality pistols, especially the 1911. Today Kimber pistols are used by the LAPD SWAT teams, the U.S. Marines, and U.S. Rapid Shooting Olympic Team members.

Kimber has seen its share of financial difficulties and buyouts. In the mid-1990s, Greg Warne, one of the original founders of Kimber, started up Kimber of America with financial backing from Les Edelman. Edelman eventually bought out Warne's shares, and combined Kimber with one of his other companies that was suffering from a loss in defense contracts, Jerico Precision Manufacturing. He merged the two companies, moving Kimber to Yonkers, New York.

Today Kimber of America continues its rich tradition producing and developing high-precision pistols and rifles for military, law enforcement, and personal use.

Compact CDP II

Custom Aegis II

Custom Covert II

Custom II

Custom Target II

Custom TLE II

Custom TLE/RL II

Desert Warrior

Kimber

Eclipse Custom II

Eclipse Pro II

Eclipse Pro Target II

Eclipse Ultra II

Gold Combat II

Gold Combat RL II

Gold Combat Stainless II

Gold Match II

Grand Raptor II

Pro TLE/RL II

Pro Aegis II

Pro Carry HD II

Pro Carry II

Pro CDP II

Pro Covert II

Pro Crimson Carry II

Pro TLE II

Raptor II

Rimfire Super

Rimfire Target Silver

Rossi

Amadeo Rossi established the Rossi Company in 1889. The founder's goal was to produce an affordable product without giving up an accuracy or quality in Sao Paolo, Brazil.

In 1997, in order to better control their sales, Rossi set up BrazTech International, L.C., as an exclusive importer of Rossi products in North America.

Rossi is known for the production of revolvers, single-shot rifles, muzzleloaders, and lever-action rifles. In 2003 Rossi was honored with the awards of "Best of the Best" and "Best Value" from *Field & Stream* magazine for its Rossi Trifecta. The versatile Trifecta is like three guns in one, as the system includes barrels for a .243 Winchester, 22 Long Rifle, and a 20-gauge shotgun.

Today Rossi is still in the hands of the original family.

Matched Pair Pistol 410Ga/45LC & 22LR 11" Blue

35102 38 Special

35202 38 Special

46102 .357 Magnum 2"

85104 38 Special
+ P 6-Shot

97206 .357 Magnum 6"

97104 .357 Magnum 4"

Ruger

Ruger (the common name for Sturm, Ruger & Co.) is the largest maker of firearms in the United States, as well as one of the few to make all three major lines of firearms: handguns, shotguns and rifles.. Their corporate motto is, "Arms Makers for Responsible Citizens."

Founded by William B. Ruger and Alexander McCormick Sturm in 1949 in a small rented machine shop in Southport, Connecticut, it first produced a well-received 22 caliber pistol. Some of the design features of the pistol came out of Ruger's earlier work studying and adapting techniques from two Baby Nambu pistols he had gotten from a US Marine who had brought them home from Japan after World War II. Although the company decided not to market the actual pistols, they did use the Nambu's rear style cocking device and silhouette in the concept for the .22 caliber pistols.

Ruger has been an important manufacturer of the .22 rimfire rifle with their popular Ruger 10/22. Sales can be credited to its relative low cost and good quality combined with a large number of accessories and available parts. Ruger also has a large share of the 22 rimfire semi-automatic pistol market.

In 1951, Alex Sturm died, and the company continued to be run by William B. Ruger until his death in 2002. Since 1969, Sturm, Ruger has been a public company and, in 1990, became a New York Stock Exchange company.

Over the 55 year period between 1949 and 2004, Ruger produced and marketed more than 20 million firearms. Today Ruger manufactures and distributes a wide range of firearms for use in hunting, target shooting, self-defense, collecting, and law enforcement

KSR40

LC9

LCP-CT

SR22

KP345PR

KBSR9

MKIII Hunter

LCP Centerfire

KP90

22/45 Bull Barrel Rimfire

22/45 Slab Sided Rimfire

Mark III Rimfire Hunter

Gp100 4"

LCR Double Action

Redhawk .45 4"

Ruger

SP101 .327 Federal

SP101 .22 LR

Super Redhawk 7"

Bisley Vaquero .357

Bearcat Alloy Steel

Blackhawk Convertible

Vaquero .357 11"

SIG Sauer

The beginnings of the SIG Sauer firm began more than 150 years ago in 1853 in Rhone Falls, Switzerland, when Friedrich Peyer im Hof, Heinrich Moser, and Conrad Neher opened a wagon factory in the small town. They built one of the most modern factories of its day devoted to building wagons and railroad cars. After just seven years, they entered into a competition to develop a modern rifle for the Swiss Army. They won a contract from the army for 30,000 muzzle-loading Prelaz-Burnand rifles and promptly changed the company name to the Swiss Industrial Company: Schweizerische Industrie-Gesellschaft, known as SIG.

Up until the beginning of World War II, Sauer mainly manufactured shotguns and hunting rifles. During the war, they produced the Sauer 38H, a small automatic pistol.

In the 1970s, SIG wanted to work on a pistol that would balance cost with quality. By Swiss law, there are limits on the ability of Swiss companies to manufacture firearms, mandating that a Swiss company must partner with a foreign firm. SIG chose to join with the German firm of Sauer & Sohn, and the SIG Sauer series of handguns began with the SIG Sauer SIG P220 handgun in 1975. Up until the beginning of

World War II, Sauer mainly manufactured shotguns and hunting rifles. During the war, they produced the Sauer 38H, a small automatic pistol.

The year 1985 saw the creation of SIGARMS, the American branch of SIG in Tysons Corner, Virginia. The divisions was established in order to import the P220 and P230 semiautomatic handguns. In 1987, SIGARMS moved to Herndon, Virginia, and then to Exeter, New Hampshire, in 1990.

In October of 2002, Michael Lüke and Thomas Ortmeier took over SIGARMS, and its European sister companies, Sauer & Sohn, Blaser, Mauser, and Swiss Arms. SIG Sauer, the largest of the five companies, is one of the major firearms producers in the world. As far as its growth in the United States, it has expanded sales more than 50 percent since 2005.

SIGARMS changed its name officially to SIG Sauer in October 2007. Most recently, the U.S. Coast Guard awarded SIG Sauer a contract to produce their standard issue firearm, and the Office of Homeland Security and Customs Enforcement also has signed them on as one of their exclusive arms suppliers.

P220 Elite Platinum

P220 Carry Elite Black

P224 SAS Nitron

P220 Carry Elite Stainless

P220 Combat

P220 Equinox

P220 Scorpian

SIG Sauer

P226 X5

P226 DAK

P226 Enhanced Elite

P229 22LR

P229 DAK

P239 Two-Tone

1911 STX

1911 Scorpion

SIG Sauer

.357 Magnum

1911 Compact C3

SP2022

SP2022 Black Diamond Plate

Mosquito Reversed Two-Tone

Mosquito Sport

P220 Classic 22

P226 X5 SCANDIC Golden Dragon

SIG Sauer

P226 Classic 22

P226 Elite Dark

P229 Elite Stainless

P232 Stainless

P238 Nitron

P250 Full Size

Smith & Wesson

In 1852 two New Englanders, Horace Smith and Dan Wesson, joined forces to found the Smith & Wesson Company. Smith had learned about firearms while working at the National Armory in Springfield, Massachusetts. Wesson's experience was gleaned from his years as an apprentice to his brother, Edwin, a famous maker of target pistols and rifles. They opened a facility in Norwich, Connecticut, to design and produce lever–action repeating pistols with fully self-contained cartridges. This did not prove to be a success, and in 1854 they sold the company to a shirt manufacturer, Oliver Winchester, who went on (in 1866) to use their design as the basis for his Winchester Repeating Arms Company.

The two men tried again in 1856, forming a partnership to produce a revolver to fire the rimfire cartridge. This became the earliest fully self-contained revolver available in the world. Smith & Wesson held the patents preventing others from producing similar firearms.

Their next design was ready for market in 1870—the Model 3 American, the first large caliber cartridge revolver. They also gained two major new clients for the .357 weapon: the United States Cavalry and the Russian Imperial Army.

Toward the end of the century, Smith retired, selling his shares in the firm to Wesson. The company soon introduced a line of hammerless revolvers that are still produced today.

Possibly the most famous contribution of Smith & Wesson was the .38 Military & Police or the Model 10. In continual production since its inception, the Model 10 is used by nearly every police and military force in existence.

In 1935 Smith & Wesson continued to add both to their product line and their worldwide reputation with the development and manufacture of the first Magnum revolver, the .375. Later, in 1955, they followed with the production of the Model 39.

Perhaps the most well-known Magnum in the line was introduced in 1956—the .44 Magnum used by Clint Eastwood in his role as *Dirty Harry*. The first stainless steel Magnum, Model 60, was first produced in 1965.

Today, in addition to its lengthy register of renowned firearms, the Smith & Wesson brand produces bicycles, gun accessories, handcuffs, safes, clothing, collectibles, knives, tools, air guns, cologne, and handbags—among many other items.

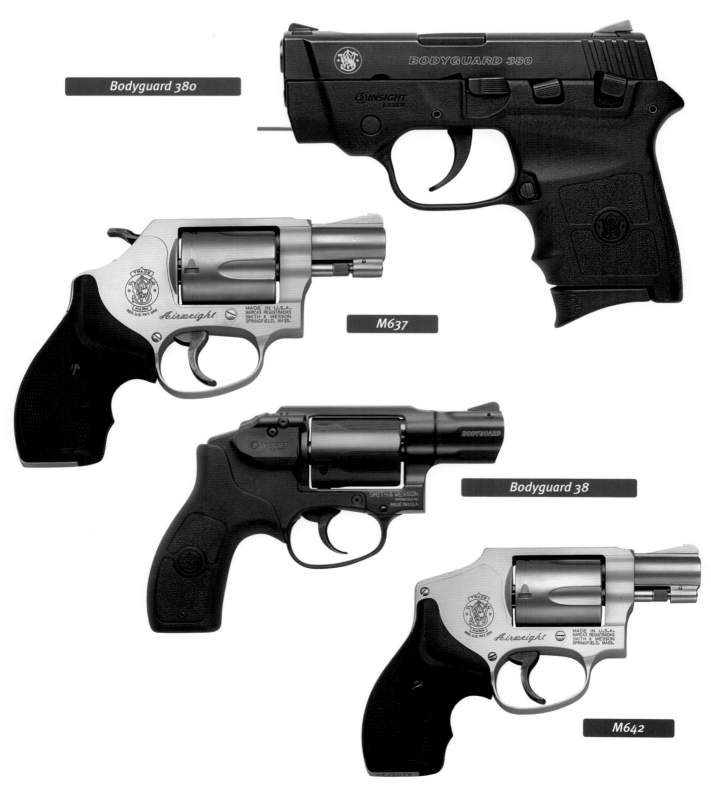

Bodyguard 380

M637

Bodyguard 38

M642

Model 27 .357 Magnum
Anniversary Edition

SD40

SMITH & WESSON SD40

SMITH & WESSON SD9

SD9

Model 36 Engraved

M&P 340 CT

Classic 586 4"

Smith & Wesson

SW1911

SW1911 CT - "E" Series

SW1911Sc

SW1911TA - "E" Series

PCModel 46oXVR

M&P .45

M&P .357

Smith & Wesson

M&P .40

M&P 9mm

M22A

M41

M410

M457

M908

M910S

Smith & Wesson

M410S

MSW40VE

M3913LS

MSW9GVE

M945S

M952

MSW990L

MSW1911 Stainless

MSW1911 Black

MSW1911PD

Smith & Wesson

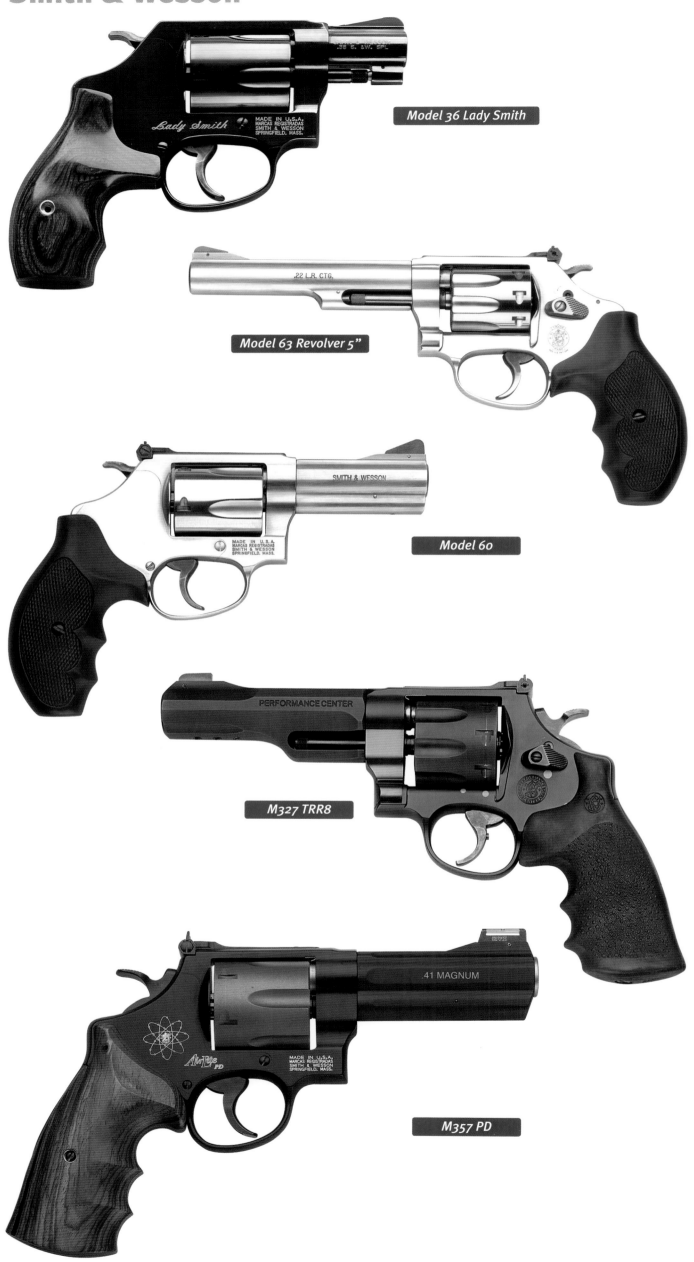

Model 36 Lady Smith

Model 63 Revolver 5"

Model 60

M327 TRR8

M357 PD

M340

M629

M637

M&P 340 CT

M629 Classic

Springfield Armory

Established in 1794 in Springfield, Massachusetts, Springfield Armory was opened under the authority of George Washington during the Revolutionary War. It became the first U.S. National Armory and was used for the manufacturing, testing, storage, repair, and development of military small arms, including muskets and rifles. Despite being a pioneer of firearms and firearm manufacturing methods, Springfield Armory was closed in 1968 after 174 years of U.S. government service.

The legendary name "Springfield Armory" was trademarked by Elmer C. Balance, owner of LH Manufacturing in San Antonio, Texas. Forefronting the company's success in 1974 was the production of the first civilian M14 rifle, the M1A rifle. However, amidst its increasing popularity, Balance sold Springfield Armory to Robert Reese, a man with a well-established production shop and firearms experience. Reese expanded the company's market with the production of the notable M1911 pistol.

The Springfield Armory Company, now located in Geneseo, Illinois, is run by Robert Reese's two sons Dennis and Tom. They continued to gain success by branching into many other fields of firearms, offering clones of M1 Garand rifles, Beretta BM59, FN FAL, HK 91, and AR-15, also importing Tanfoglio and Astra

semiautomatic pistols under the Springfield name. However, the company's main products still remain the M1911 pistol (built using Brazilian components produced by IMBEL) and the M1A semiautomatic rifle series.

Springfield Armory also has a well-known custom shop headed by gunsmith David Williams, with well-known previous directors including Les Baer and Jack Weigand. Full-custom M1911A1s and semicustom XD pistols are built and modified here, as well as their most famous product, the Tactical Response Pistol Professional Model (formerly known as the Bureau Model). The TRP Professional was one of only two guns to pass the controversial trials set forth by the Federal Bureau of Investigation for a new pistol for its Hostage Rescue Team and SWAT teams.

Today the Springfield Armory proudly bares the motto "the first name in American firearms," a reference to its historical name trademarked from the original Springfield Armory in Springfield, Massachusetts.

Among the company's noted accomplishments is also the inception of the practical shooting team in 1985, where Rob Leatham is captain of Team Springfield.

PI9128LP Range Officer

P19209 LP 3" EMP

XD Tactical Model 5"

XD40 Pro Carry

PB9108L

PB9114L

PC9105L

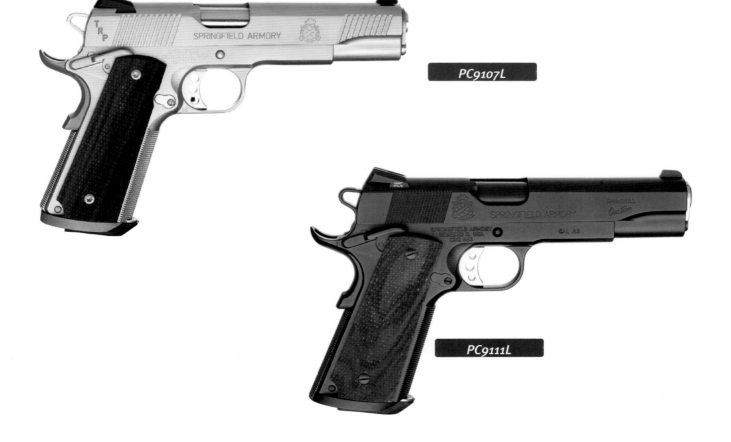

PC9107L

PC9111L

PC9206

PC9802L

PI9134L

XD9101

XD9401

XD9515

XDm Compact 3.8" .45

Springfield Armory

XD9524

XD9701

XD9801F

XD9505

XD9811

XD9821

Taurus

Forjas Taurus (Taurus Forge) was a small tool manufacturer established in Porto Alegre, Brazil, in 1939. The company produced its first revolver in 1941, the Model 38101SO. The revolver incorporated many elements from other competitive gun manufactures of the day including, Colt and Smith & Wesson. Following its production, Taurus was recognized as an emerging adversary in the South American gun market.

In 1968 Taurus, interested in expanding their gun production and market, became a publicly traded company. Allowing Bangor Punta, an American conglomerate, to purchase 54 percent of the shares in 1970. Bangor Punta also owned another well-known firearms production company—Smith & Wesson. Over the next seven years, now sister companies, Taurus and Smith & Wesson began sharing technology and methodology, resulting in improved manufacturing. However, in 1977 Taurus regained its independence by buying back the 54 percent share from Bangor Punta.

The now-independent Taurus arms company seized an opportunity to expand in the Brazilian market. In 1980 they purchased a gun manufacturing plant in São Paulo from Beretta, an Italian-based gun manufacturer. Beretta had been contracted in 1974 to produce firearms for the Brazilian army, and due to the terms of their contract constructed the gun plant in São Paulo. Along with the purchase of the plant, Taurus gained everything that once belonged to Beretta, including drawings, tooling, machinery, and a very experienced work force. Being in the pistol business already, Taurus began to improve upon the Beretta pistol design, resulting in the production of the acclaimed Taurus PT-92 and PT-99 9 mm pistols.

In 1982 Taurus expanded yet again, opening an affiliate company in Miami, Florida. Without having a solid distribution system established or proper press recognition in America, Taurus needed an aggressive marketing campaign.

At the Dallas, Texas, S.H.O.T. Show in 1984, Taurus announced its lifetime repair policy. Forefronting the entire firearm industry with this policy changed the course of the company's success. Since initiating this innovative marketing strategy, Taurus has become one of the largest small arms manufacturers in the world.

405

638 PRO

DT Hybrid

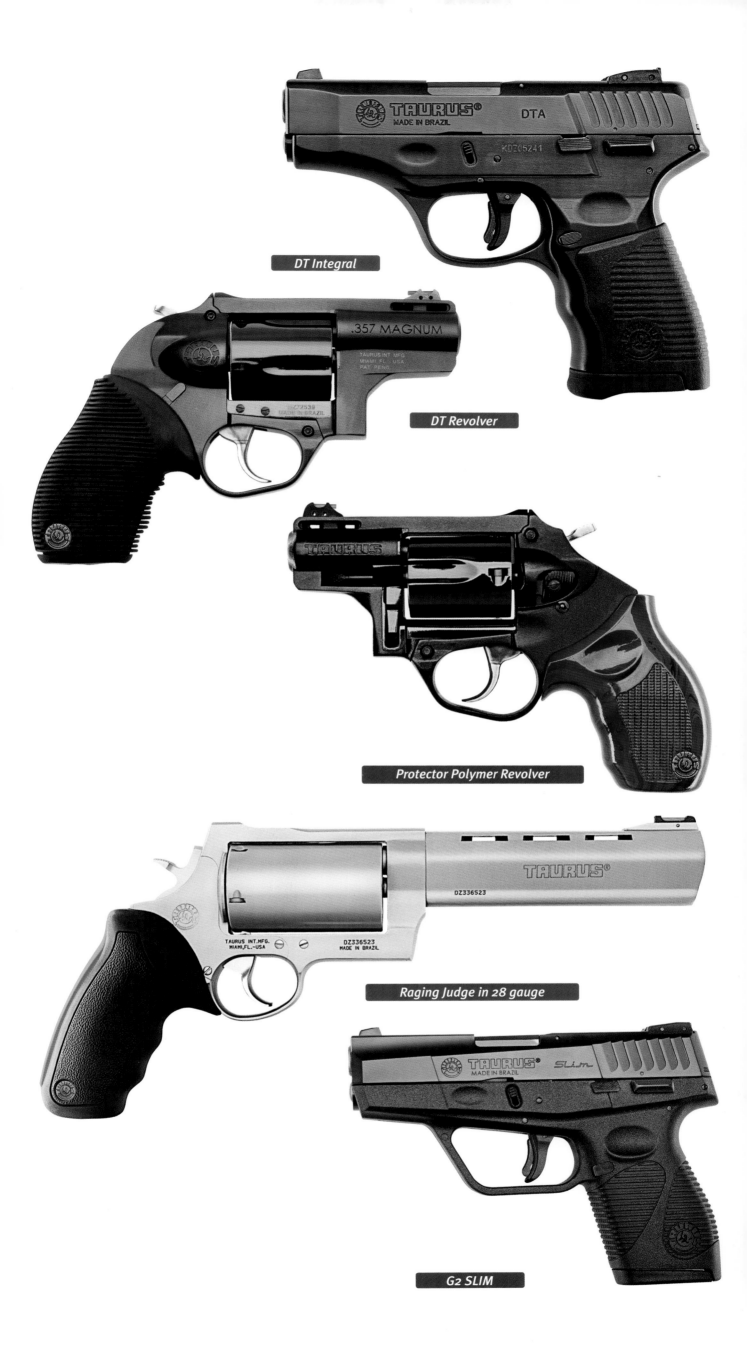

DT Integral

DT Revolver

Protector Polymer Revolver

Raging Judge in 28 gauge

G2 SLIM

Taurus

SA 45

PT 809

PT 1911

617BT

817 Stainless Steel

PT 24/7 Pro

PT 24/7 Pro C

SA 45 Stainless

Taurus

SA 357

92B

99 Stainless Steel

24/7-G29B

Taurus

100 Stainless Steel

101B

44 Stainless 8

738 TCP

608 SS 6

38S

58HCS

845

Taurus

909B

911 Stainless Steel

940

TRACKER MODEL 17

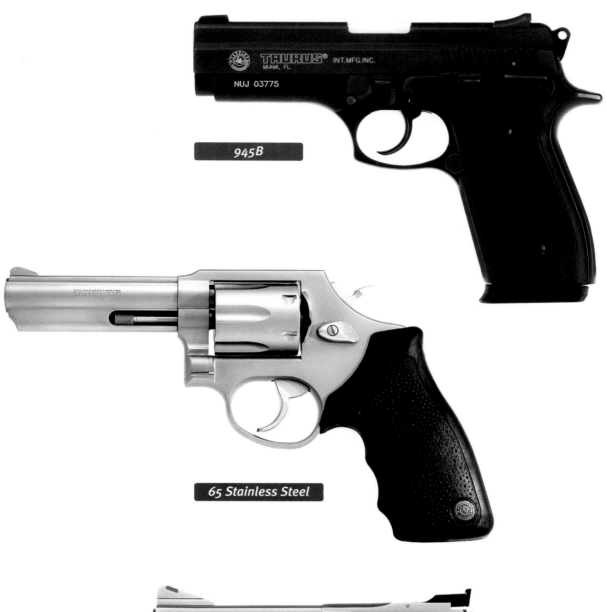

945B

65 Stainless Steel

66 Stainless Steel

Protector Polymer

Taurus

82 B 4

Millennium Pro Titanium 111

Raging Bull 444

.38 Special +P

605 B2

444 Ultra-Lite Titanium Blue

4510 TKR

Public Defender Polymer

Thompson/Center

Thompson/Center Arms Company was set up in 1965 when a convenient colloboration between K. W. Thompson Tool Company, which was seeking new products to fill its production capabilities, partnered with Warren Center, a gun designer in search of a manufacturer for his Contender pistol. Thompson Tool facilities were expanded and the new company Thompson/Center, was formed in Rochester, New Hampshire. It took only two years for the first Contender pistols to ship, and the company has been producing hunting handguns ever since. Today, Thompson/Center has marketed more than 400,000 of these pistols.

Two years later, the first contender pistol was shipped, starting a trend in high-performance hunting handguns, which continues to grow every year. To date, over 400,000 Contender pistols have been shipped and the pistol's reputation for versatility, accuracy, and dependability goes unchallenged among serious handgun shooters.

The company became known for its line of interchangeable barrel single-shot pistols and rifles. The company has also helped spur a resurgance of interest in muzzle-loading rifles, which they began manufacturing in 1970 with the introduction of the Hawken muzzleloading rifle.

In the present day, Thompson/Center's product line includes single-shot pistols and rifles, and a full line of muzzleloading rifles and accessories. The original version of the Contender pistol has been updated as the G2 Contender and is one of the best-known hunting handguns available today.

Encore 1626

G2 Contender 2702

Pistol Hunters Package

Encore 1628

G2 Contender 2720

G2 Contender 3556

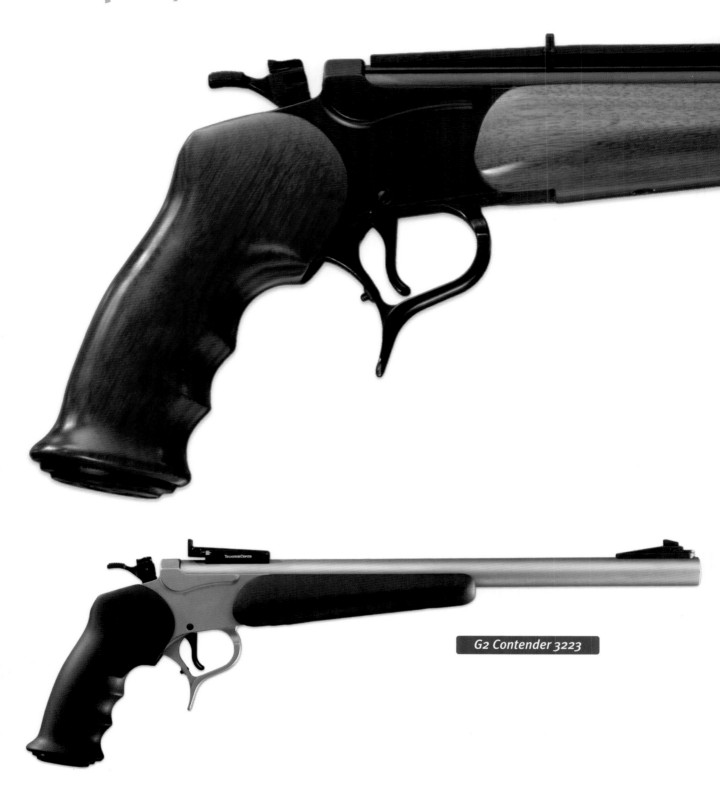

G2 Contender 3223

Encore 5849

G2 Contender 3566

Encore 5870

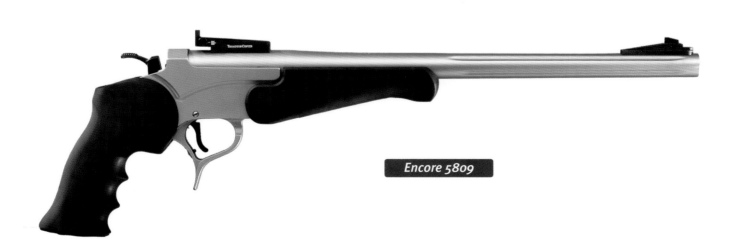

Encore 5809

Uberti

A. Uberti, S.r.l. was established in 1959 by Aldo Uberti in the Italian Alps foothill village of Gardone Val Trompia. The company is a daughter to the well-known Beretta firearms company and resides within the Beretta industrial complex.

Dedicated to creating high-quality replicas, Uberti took his first project in 1959 reproducing the 1851 Navy Colt in commemoration of the 100th anniversary of the American Civil War, positively establishing the company's reputation. The continued popularity of their reproductions led to the manufacturing of the 1866 Winchester lever-action replica in 1965 as well as the Colt Single-Action Army replica called "Cattleman" in 1966.

Movie directors began consulting Aldo Uberti to reproduce guns for Western films. In 1960, well-known Italian movie director Sergio Leone was the first to use Uberti Old West replicas in his series of Western films, which later would come to be known as "spaghetti westerns." These movie sets, featuring characters clad with Uberti replica firearms, sparked an international fascination with Italian-made guns. Among the Western films contributing to the Uberti replica notoriety are popular films such as *The Outlaw Josey Wales*, *A Fistful of Dollars* trilogy, *Dances with Wolves*, and *Tombstone*.

Uberti is currently the world's largest reproducer of historical American firearms, manufacturing about 30,000 handguns and 10,000 rifles annually. They employ about sixty skilled artisans to fit and assemble the precisely cast and cut parts as they come off the computer numerical control machinery. With the fast-growing Civil War and Western reenactment industry, Uberti replica firearms have become a staple to the gun manufacturing industry.

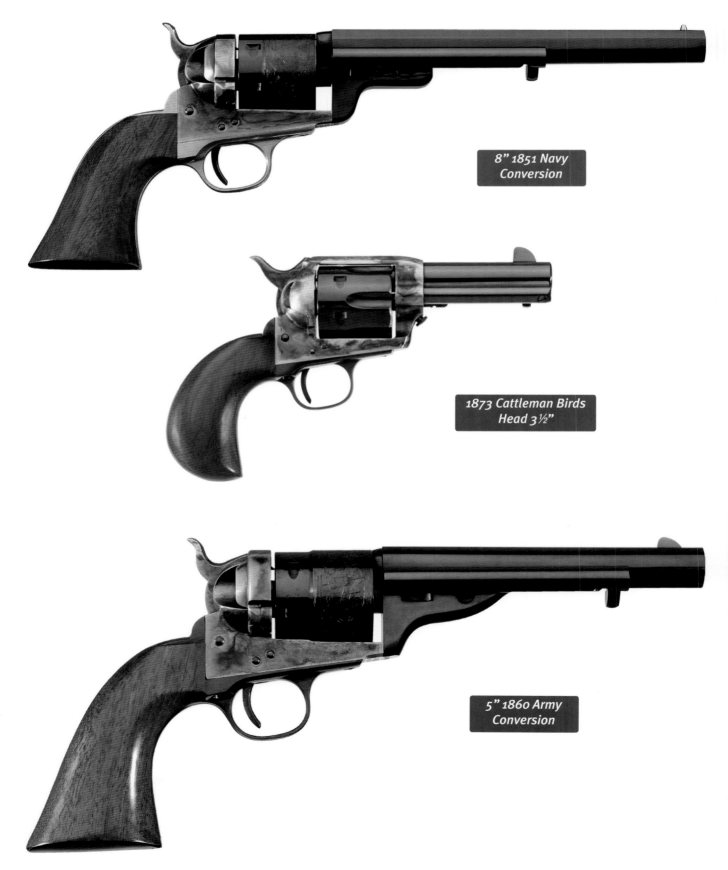

8" 1851 Navy Conversion

1873 Cattleman Birds Head 3½"

5" 1860 Army Conversion

1871–72 Late Model Open Top

1875 Frontier 5½"

1875 Outlaw 7½"

1890 Police 5½"

Uberti

1873 Cattleman Bisley 7½"

Rolling Block Pistol

1873 Cattleman Steel NM 4¾"

Engraved Top Break 7"

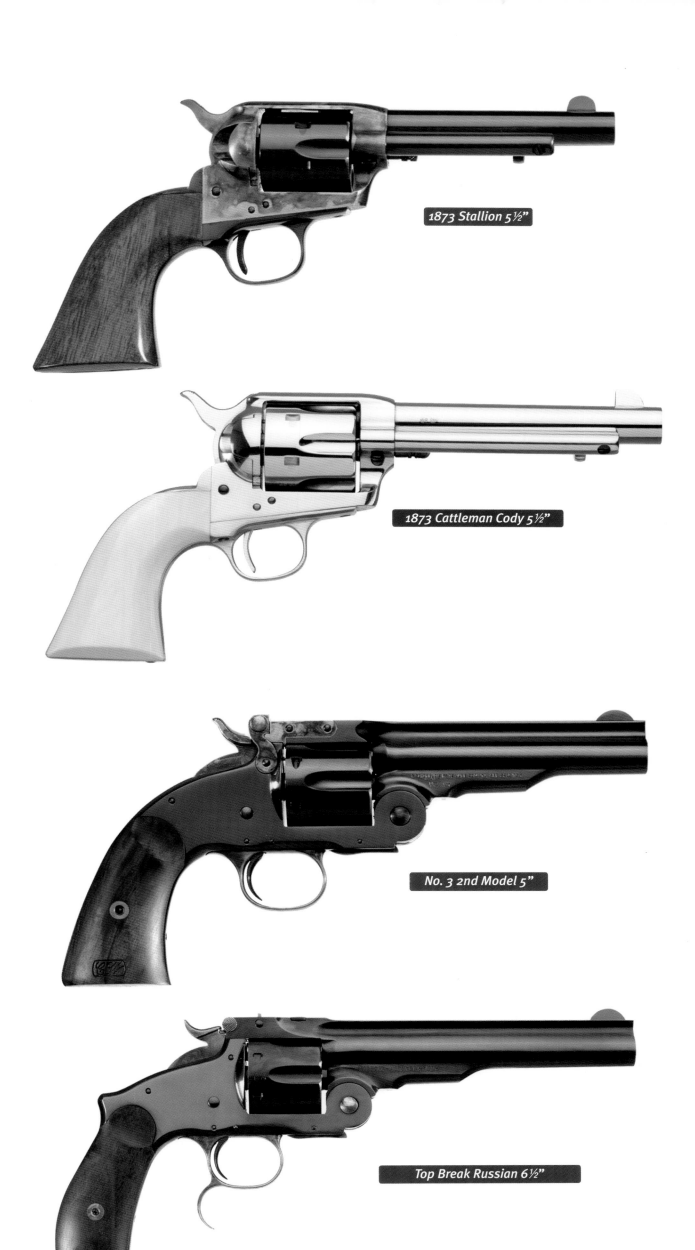

1873 Stallion 5½"

1873 Cattleman Cody 5½"

No. 3 2nd Model 5"

Top Break Russian 6½"

U.S. Fire Arms

United States Fire Arms Manufacturing Company, Inc. (USFA) is the only gun manufacturer who still has its factory in Hartford, Connecticut. USFA produces mainly single-action revolvers associated with the late nineteenth century in the United States. Even the location of the factory is tied to the company's product line; it is set up "under the Blue Dome," once the home of the Colt East Armory where Colt Manufacturing Company built classic firearms in the late nineteenth and early twentieth centuries.

The designs may be traditional and historical, but the production techniques are state of the art using modern computer numerical controlled machine technology. All of their firearms are produced entirely in the United States. USFA's reputation is based on their production of the Colt Single-Action Army revolver. U.S. Fire Arms also produces and markets semiautomatic M1911 pistols, the Ace .22LR conversion, and the Lightning rifle. Since 2007, Remington Arms Company has reached a licensing deal with U.S. Fire Arms to manufacture a line of historically correct reproductions.

1910 Commercial

1881 Flattop Target

.22 Plinker

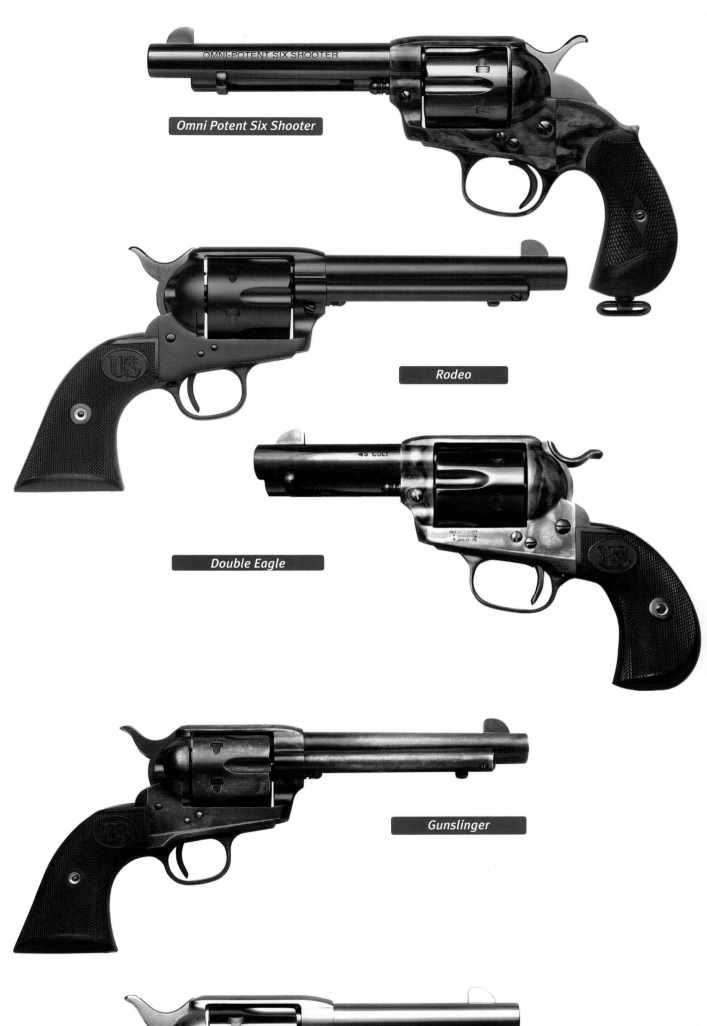

Omni Potent Six Shooter

Rodeo

Double Eagle

Gunslinger

Sheriff

Walther

In 1886 Carl Walther opened his first production facility for Walther Works in Zella-Mehlis, Thuringia, in Germany, an area famous for its gunmakers. In 1908 Walther's concept was to build a self-loading handgun; he marketed the first German self-loading Walther Model 1, caliber 6.35 mm. In World War I, almost every German soldier was issued a Walther pocket gun.

Carl Walther died in 1915, and was succeeded in the business by his son Fritz who kept honing the self-loading technology. In 1929 Fritz made the first single-/double-action trigger pistol, the Walther Model PP. This was soon followed by a compact model PPK. In 1938, at the request of the German military, Walther developed a more powerful version with the 9 mm cartridge in the Model P38. The classic design of this gun is still used today and imitated by many firearms makers.

During World War II, the Walther factory was destroyed. Fritz managed to salvage some of the design plans, however, and brought them with him to West Germany after the end of the war. By 1953 he had completed building a new factory in the city of Ulm along the banks of the Danube in Germany. The main Walther factory is still there today.

In 1993 Walther merged with Umarex and expanded their reach on a more global basis. In the 1996 Summer Olympics in Atlanta, Georgia, Walther pistols were used by some of the gold medalists. Together they have produced the Model 99, nicknamed "the First Pistol of the Next Century," which is mainly used by police and military forces.

Q-style P22

PPQ

PPK Engraved

P22 Black Target

P22 Target Nickel Military

P22 Target Military

P99 AS

Walther

P22

P22 Military

P22 Nickel

P22 Anthracite

PK380 Bi-color

PK380 Black

PK380 Laser

Walther

P99c QA

PPK Blue

PPK/S Crimson Trace

P99 QA

PPK Stainless

PPK/S Blue

Walther

PPK/S Stainless

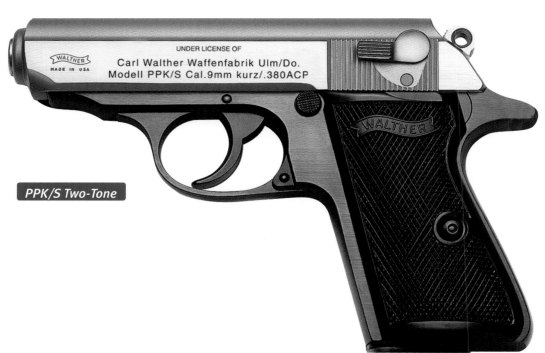

PPK/S Two-Tone

SP22 M1

SP22 M2

SP22 M3

SP22 M4

Index